UNIVERSITY OF WALES   BOARD OF CELTIC STUDIES

SOCIAL SCIENCE MONOGRAPHS

General Editor: Harold Carter, Gregynog Professor of Human Geography
University College of Wales, Aberystwyth

Number 3

ATTITUDES AND SECOND HOMES
IN RURAL WALES

by

CHRIS BOLLOM

Cardiff
University of Wales Press
1978

© UNIVERSITY OF WALES PRESS 1978

ISBN 0 7083 0659 4

PRINTED IN
WALES BY
A. McLAY & CO. LTD.
CARDIFF

CONTENTS

LIST OF TABLES

iii

PREFACE

A SOCIOLOGICAL STUDY OF SECOND HOMES IN NORTH WALES

Second-home ownership has become a controversial issue in recent years and although a great deal of statistical material has been gathered by local authority planning departments and other bodies concerned with the economic and social development of rural areas little work has been done on the social and cultural aspects of second-home ownership in Welsh-speaking communities. It is a truism that the Welsh language and the traditional Welsh way of life survive most robustly in the rural areas of Gwynedd. It is therefore in these areas that one would expect to find the impact of second-home ownership by English immigrants from the North and the Midlands is greatest thereby producing the greatest degree of hostility on the part of native Welsh residents. The purpose of this inquiry was to find whether and in what degree this hostility was generated. Or to put the matter in more technical language – the purpose was to test the hypothesis that the invasion of occasional residence in Welsh-speaking communities creates a situation of stress and whether it could be assumed that the greater the density of second homes in such communities the more intense would be the inter-group tensions generated. Certain relevant variables in such a situation would have to be isolated and identified, such as the scatter of second homes in relation to the focal settlement, i.e., whether they were spread out on the periphery of the community or concentrated in the centre of the village, whether the immigrants formed colonies among the native residents and were and felt themselves to be isolated in the community, and to what extent the natives regarded the incomers not merely as different to themselves in language and behaviour but potentially destructive to their traditional way of life.

The Social Science Committee of the Board of Celtic Studies of the University of Wales appointed Mr. Christopher Bollom to conduct an inquiry into this field. As he had only 12 months to make his investigations and to prepare a report it was obviously necessary to limit the number of communities in which such a study could be made in depth. Five such communities were chosen because they all had a significant number of second homes in varying proportions to their total size and differed in the location of those homes, some were in the centre of the village, others scattered on the countryside outside the village. They were Penmachno, Cwm Penmachno, Croesor, Rhiw (in the Lleyn peninsula) and Llansannan. The latter is in Clwyd but is a good example of an inland village settlement where most second homes are on the outskirts or at some distance from the village itself. The three first-mentioned villages are inland villages where the decline of the slate quarries has resulted in many of the original inhabitants leaving the area and where a number of houses would have become derelict were it not for their purchase by second-home owners. Rhiw is an upland village but near to the sea and the coastal resort of Pwllheli, with easy access to the beaches of the Lleyn peninsula, and therefore a place which has obvious attractions to tourists and holidaymakers.

Mr. Bollom used the usual techniques of such social surveys, a postal questionnaire, a follow-up face-to-face interview which was carefully structured and in which he was assisted by a number of Welsh-speaking postgraduate students. Unfortunately, some members of these communities had received requests for information from a variety of other investigators over recent years and were understandably reluctant to answer a series of questions yet again. But with few exceptions most of those who were approached were willing to co-operate.

Mr. Bollom gives a more detailed account of his methods and findings in the following report. One of his major conclusions can be anticipated. Contrary to his (and others') expectations it was not the *density* of second-home ownership which was the most provocative factor in the situation. Contrary to his expectations he was not able to discover a 'cut-off' point where tolerance towards second homes became converted to hostility where their numbers increased. In Rhiw which has proportionately the greatest saturation of second homes there is less evidence of inter-group tension. In Llansannan, however, where the numbers are proportionately fewer, a number of local people felt threatened and their attitude therefore is more critical. Mr. Bollom points out therefore that the significant factor is not number and density alone. The nature of local leadership patterns in the community, the vitality of local village life and the influence of the traditional institutions of that village life like the chapel and the school are all significant factors. The effects of high density ownership would not appear to be uniform.

Since second-home owners do not participate in the services of the chapel which are conducted in Welsh, and since their children, if they only visit their second home at holiday times, do not go to the local school, they are not seen as 'belonging'. In Rhiw a chapel and school have now closed. If high density of second homes is not by itself a factor in producing a hostile reaction in the native inhabitants, it must be stated that under certain conditions when the density of second homes reaches a certain level the traditional cultural institutions may become submerged and the relationship between the social groups becomes one of accommodation and acceptance. This is not an argument for promoting high density of second homes nor is it a sequence which invariably occurs. It is merely a factual statement of what can happen when the proportion of second homes becomes so high as to bring about radical changes (with other social causes) in the traditional pattern of Welsh village life.

H. MORRIS-JONES

ACKNOWLEDGEMENTS

The research upon which this report is based was sponsored by the Board of Celtic Studies of the University of Wales and the Social Science Research Council, to whom I extend my grateful thanks.

The project would not have been completed without the help of a number of people in the Department of Social Theory and Institutions at the University College of North Wales, Bangor. I would like to thank Professor Huw Morris-Jones for his continuing encouragement and patience while this report was being compiled, and for his concern and interest during the whole project. I must express my gratitude to Mr. John Borland and Dr. Glyn Williams for their help and the benefit of their experience which was given so freely. The fieldwork would not have been completed without the help of a doughty trio of interviewers, Gerry Evans, Catrin Roberts and Tecwyn Vaughan Jones, who tell me that their command of the Welsh language improved greatly during their conversations with the people of the villages we studied. Finally, I must thank Miss Delyth Howells for her patience and skill in transforming an untidy manuscript into a well-presented document. Any errors and mistakes which remain are, of course, my own.

CHRIS BOLLOM

DEFINITION

Whatever else its failings this report makes little contribution to the question of the definition of a second home. Perhaps the two factors of definition which have caused the most difficulty have been the question of whether flats, chalets and especially caravans should be regarded as second homes, and whether a definition should include specific mention of the use to which a second home is put. The present study utilized the following definition of a second home:

> A property which is owned, leased or rented and which is available for the exclusive use, over a twelve-month period, of a family unit whose normal daily journey time is minimized at another residence.[1]

We failed to find a caravan or chalet which could have been regarded as a second home in any of the villages studied, and although very few second homes were in fact rented, where this was the case the rentees invariably had sole use of the property throughout the year.

(1) See reference 7, Chapter One, pp. 1–8.

CHAPTER 1

INTRODUCTION

The numbers of second homes in Britain are not known with any certainty, and published statistics give no indication of the extent of second-home ownership in the country. In contrast, other countries have long been statistically aware of second homes[1] and in the United States and France where its inclusion in the national census is taken for granted it is estimated that 5% and 11% respectively of households own second homes. In Denmark this figure is approximately 10% while in Sweden, where the subject has been investigated by detailed national survey, it rises to 20%. The general consensus of opinion suggests that built second homes in England and Wales number between 160–200,000, but to this figure must be added some 150,000 static caravans. This gives a total estimate of second homes in England and Wales of 300–350,000 implying that some 2% of households own a second home, a considerably lower proportion than in most other European countries. It is estimated that this figure has been growing by about 25,000 a year in recent years with built second homes growing more rapidly in number than caravans.

The regional distribution of second homes is again difficult to establish accurately. The D.A.R.T. report on second homes prepared for the Countryside Commission quotes the Audits of Great Britain Limited[2] estimate that the South East of England with 23% of built second homes and 25% of caravan second homes in the country has the highest proportion of both types of second homes. The South West of England is the next highest in aggregate with 20% of the built second homes and 16% of the caravans, just above Wales with 15.9% of the built second homes and 19.5% of the caravans. These three regions contain between them nearly 60% of the country's second homes compared with only 39% of the housing stock, and in Wales the proportion of second homes rises to 2.7 times the proportion of the national housing stock, 2.4 times if caravans are excluded. The three big urbanized areas of the East and West Midlands and the North West of England are regarded as regions which export second-home owners in contrast to the South West of England and Wales which appear to be importing regions.

The distribution of built second homes within England and Wales has been influenced by a number of factors. The dominant impression is that most of the present stock of built second homes has been created by a change of use of existing dwellings. They are set within the local settlement pattern, their place being dictated as much by the ceasing of first home use through economic decline as by any specific search for location by the second-home owner. This pattern of second-home growth following first-home decline does much to explain the great variation in the density of second homes throughout England and Wales and in specific areas. Clearly areas affected by economic decline where there is or has been little locally generated demand for housing have tended to attract an influx of second-home buyers, while the importance of ready access is reflected in the numbers of second homes to be found in proximity to the major conurbations.

The D.A.R.T. report concludes that some 15.9% of the built second homes are located in Wales, approximately 26,000 based on a total figure of 160,000. Table 1 indicates the available data concerning the distribution of this total among the old counties of Wales, based on figures derived from the County Planning Departments concerned. An important point worth noting is that over 50% of the estimated number of second homes in Wales is not accounted for by these eight rural counties. Assuming the estimates to be correct a significant number of second homes must be located in the new county of Powys (excluding Montgomery), the old county of Flint in the north, and the Glamorgans and Gwent in the south. However, these counties are reported by the Wye College Report [3] to contain only between 0–7% of their sample distribution of second homes in Wales. Possibly this is due to an overestimation of the number of second homes in the Principality or to an underestimation of the numbers in the eight old counties for which statistics are available, but there remains the somewhat puzzling question of the distribution of the remainder.

Table 1
Second Homes in Rural Wales

County	Permanent built second homes	Proportion of housing stock	Percentage of Welsh total 26,000
Caernarfon	2,980	7%	11.5%
Anglesey	2,224	14%	8.6%
Merioneth	2,200	14%	8.5%
Cardigan	1,296	4.7%	5.0%
Pembroke	1,500	figures not	5.8%
Carmarthen	393	available	1.5%
Denbigh	586	6.9%	2.3%
Montgomery	739	4.8%	2.8%
TOTALS	11,918		46%

SOURCE: County Planning Departments.

NOTE: The total for Denbighshire is based on data for the four Rural Districts of Aled, Ceiriog, Hiraethog and Ruthin.

A number of planning departments in Wales have investigated the second-home situation in their areas. Reports have been published by Caernarfonshire[4], Denbighshire[5] and Merioneth[6], and some other smaller scale examinations of the position in Wales as well as some statistics for other of the old counties are available. The county reports have provided information concerning the second home itself, their number, type and distribution, their owners' origin, intensity of use of the dwelling and the reasons for their choice of second-home location, and the costs and benefits of second-home ownership to the receiving area. The source base for the surveys is the District Council's rating registers, the number of non-local ratepayers being the starting point. However, rating lists can include non-local ratepayers who are not second-home owners and exclude owners whose rate demands are sent direct to the second home. For this reason, much follow-up work is required, including door-to-door surveys of selected localities to determine an appropriate percentage figure by which rating register numbers should be increased to provide a more accurate estimate. In his report on Second Homes in North Wales[7], Richard de Vane argues that these methods used to gross up to a county figure from detailed surveys of selected areas can be quite inaccurate and that the numbers of second homes in Gwynedd (Anglesey, Caernarfon and Merioneth) may have been overestimated, further complicating the issue of the numbers of second homes in Wales. All the surveys faced problems of definition, but all excluded caravans from their surveys. Whilst Caernarfonshire found it impossible to exclude holiday investment and club or company holiday property, the Denbighshire definition of a second home as a dwelling intended for leisure or holiday purposes and not the usual or permanent place of residence of the owner appeared to exclude rented dwellings, but the survey did in fact include rented leasehold accommodation.

The Caernarfonshire survey estimated a total built second-home stock of some 2,980 dwellings, 7% of the total housing stock of the county, with the density of ownership varying widely between areas. Lleyn Rural District has the highest average with one parish with over 50% of second homes in its total dwellings, and although the percentage of second homes was found to be high in some inland parishes, the total numbers in coastal parishes were much higher. In Merioneth the 2,200 built second homes formed 14% of the total county dwelling stock with a concentration in the southern part of the county, the Towyn-Llangelynin area. Figures based on the 1969 rating registers in Anglesey suggest that the estimated 2,224 second homes form again about 14% of the county's housing stock with concentration in the Valley Rural District (nearly 80% of the total) in the Trearddur Bay and Rhosneigr areas.

Data for Pembrokeshire are sparse but the number of built second homes is estimated to have been between 1,250 and 1,500 in 1973, although no breakdown is available. Carmarthenshire's estimated 393 second homes are widely distributed but there is some concentration in Newcastle Emlyn Rural District, Cenarth and Llangeler parishes. In Cardiganshire, New Quay Urban District with an estimated 29% of its housing stock as second homes is most densely populated but Aberystwyth Rural District with over 30% of the county's total second homes contains numerically the most. The four Rural Districts of Denbighshire contain some 586 second homes, comprising 6.9% of all dwellings, with a widely fluctuating distribution from 0 to 16% in the parish of Llanarmon. In Montgomery the 739 second homes comprise 4.8% of the housing stock with 65% of the total divided equally between Llanfyllin and Newtown Rural Districts, although the highest density of ownership, 10.5%, is to be found in Machynlleth Rural District.

Some other information is available concerning second homes in East Monmouthshire [8] and the Gower Peninsula in West Glamorgan. In the Wye Valley it was found that eleven selected villages contained between them a total of 51 second homes, with the greatest density to be found in the popular tourist village of Symonds Yat, 30%. A total of 406 second homes were identified in Gower Rural District, concentrated in the east of the peninsula nearest Swansea. The highest numbers were located in the parish of Bishopston, but the greatest density, 52%, is to be found in the nearby parish of Penmaen.

Some valuable insights into the factors leading to second-home developments are obtained from the county reports. In Merioneth where 80% of existing built second homes are old properties, local distribution seems to have been determined by economic changes, principally the decline of employment in the slate quarries and in agriculture which has led to the availability of cottages formerly occupied by the workers engaged in these activities. A similar pattern is to be found in Caernarfonshire especially in the inland parishes, but in the Lleyn Peninsula the proportion of new dwellings is much higher, reflecting the diminishing supply of older properties and the greater density of second homes on the peninsula. In Denbighshire several factors seem to affect the proportions of second homes in parishes, notably depopulation and the quality of agricultural land, where amalgamation of farm holdings and an increasingly mechanized quarrying industry have made fewer demands for local labour.

Certainly in the cases of the North Wales counties the West Midlands and the North West of England are identified as the second-home owner exporting regions, with Caernarfon and Denbigh receiving most incomers from the North West and Merioneth from the West Midlands. A large proportion of owners claim specific links with Wales and the specific locality of their second home, and large numbers acquired their properties with retirement in mind. In Caernarfonshire nearly a third of the respondents had been born in Wales and in Carmarthen, in the south, this proportion was almost a half. In Denbighshire and Merioneth over a half of the owners claimed family links with Wales.

One important feature of second-home ownership which emerges from the Welsh surveys and from their counterparts in England is the large amount of time spent by owners in their second homes. In Carmarthenshire and Denbighshire respectively second homes were used on average for 92 and 87 days per year, whilst in Caernarfon and Merioneth this increased on average to 117 and 123 days respectively. The Wye College national sample used their second homes for an average of 90 days in the year although the local samples varied from 28 days in Devon to 80 days in Lancashire. Frequency of use seems to be related to the distance between first and second homes, ownership or tenancy of second homes and the intention to retire to the second home, and the frequency of use made by owners can have a significant bearing on the costs and benefits of second-home ownership to the receiving areas.

SOME COSTS AND BENEFITS OF SECOND HOMES

Having gathered information concerning second homes and their owners, previous research has sought to consider the costs, benefits and implications of second-home ownership. The economic benefits are tangible and fairly easily quantifiable, comprising capital spending on improvements, local expenditure on provisions and general services, and rates, where it is argued that second-home owners generally contribute substantially more in rates than the equivalent of the services they utilize, especially in the case of education and social services. Local expenditures by second-home families on provisions and general services were estimated at £375 annually in Denbighshire, £610 in Merioneth and £400 in Caernarfonshire. All three surveys used the employment multiplier recommended by the Department of Economics at the University College of North Wales, Bangor[9], converting annual second-home owner expenditure into 990 jobs, 480 jobs and 101 jobs respectively in Caernarfon, Merioneth and Denbigh. Richard de Vane estimates that the present structure of second-home ownership in Gwynedd resulted in an expenditure of £2,413,310 at 1974 prices, generating a total business turnover of £3,468,546 and creating a personal household income amounting to £778,483.

Information is provided in the reports concerning the frequently expressed accusation that the demand for second homes in many areas adversely affects the ability of local people to compete in the housing market. The D.A.R.T. report, which sees the low wage levels and the existence of differential demand mitigating this allegation, is supported in this view by the Denbighshire report. In Caer-

5

narfonshire higher prices for some types of property is felt to create a problem for many local people who wish to purchase their own home, but the report points out the danger of confusing the symptom, the inability of local people to compete in the housing market, with the cause – the lack of employment opportunities in parts of the country. In Merioneth evidence supports the suggestion that second-home demand is having a greater effect on older property, precisely that to which young people with few resources look as homes, but even so price levels for all types of property in the county are well below those in many other parts of the country and so young people are not necessarily at such a financial disadvantage. Overall, the extent of housing market competition varies greatly and appears to be strongly localised in certain towns and villages, especially those in coastal areas. The report by de Vane concluded that it was not possible to find suitably comparable areas between which differences of house prices could be assessed.

A study by Liverpool University Department of Civic Design of Second Homes in North Wales[10] examined local authority housing waiting lists in various parts of North Wales concluding that urban areas have the highest waiting lists and that actual pressures on urban districts are greatest in districts around which the rural areas are depopulating the fastest. Taking waiting lists as a percentage of total households in 1971, Machynlleth Urban District with 23% and Llanidloes Municipal Borough with 16%, in Powys, and Dolgellau in Gwynedd exhibited the highest percentage. In the rural districts of Caernarfon and Merioneth second homes in all cases exceed 50% of the waiting list. It is argued that they do provide a threat to local home ownership, and that this phenomenon will inevitably spread to the rest of Wales as the ability to buy and keep a second home spreads to more of the population.

Both the D.A.R.T. report and the Welsh county reports consider the implications of second-home ownership from the point of view of social costs and benefits. However, these examinations have been inadequate and it is the presence of this gap in knowledge which has stimulated the present study. Admitting an element of caricature in its description, the D.A.R.T. report expresses the view that much concern over second homes comes from the natural instinct of the human group to fear and feel threatened by the incursion of aliens into that group, and that a low income conservative farming group will react to 'wealthy liberal or agnostic town dwellers'[11] who are buying houses where generations of farmers have lived and are seeking to ease themselves into the community, feeling that local traditions may be eroded by the incomers' influence. Accompanying the social invasion, then, may be a degree of cultural shock. The report tries to put these fears into perspective. Social invasion is prevalent throughout society and can almost be seen as the antithesis of the industrial revolution. The pioneers of both flow and ebb are the economically able, the aware, and the better educated, migrating out of areas where their standard of living is threatened. The observation that second homes are rather the symptom of depopulation than the cause is stressed, and the positive contribution of second homes, both the economic and the social in terms of the provision of leadership and articulation is seen as more than could be expected from other forms of tourism.

The local county surveys examine some of the social costs said to arise when permanent residents are replaced by second-home owners, namely the destruction of community life, the displacement of neighbours resulting in loneliness and difficulties in time of need, and the decline in numbers attending chapel and other village functions. The reports generally point out that the problems of rural depopulation should not be blamed on the second-home owner as depopulation has for the most part resulted from the decline of basic industries over a long period. Nevertheless Caernarfonshire argue that although depopulation may in the first instance have encouraged the demand for second homes it cannot be denied that the subsequent rise in house prices made further migration possible. Despite evidence that ownership may now have reached such a level in some areas as to be causing depopulation, the report maintains that it is still valid to consider whether empty and derelict houses would add any more to community life than second homes, especially as it finds the level of local organization and club membership amongst second-home owners to be quite high.

The more serious set of social costs looked at by the North Wales reports is that which concerns the dilution of Welsh culture, the impact on the Welsh language and the lack of appreciation of Welsh country ways. The presence, albeit for only a quarter of the year, of second-home owners without such a Welsh background will tend to erode the way of life peculiar to the area. The survey results indicate a desire on the part of second-home owners to learn the language, while considerable proportions in all the reports claim to have links with Wales. Some surveys have sought the views of local people on this issue. The Wye College report estimated that only one-third of the residents of Aberystwyth Rural District considered themselves to be affected by second homes, whilst a large majority thought second homes to be a good trend. The survey in Denbighshire which involved questioning some twenty-one 'gate-keepers' of local opinion, for example ministers of religion and shopkeepers, suggested a generally less favourable attitude on behalf of local permanent residents. The Caernarfon report feels the situation to be moving in this direction with the further expected growth in the numbers of second homes in the area and concludes that where a lack of appreciation of Welsh country ways exists, it is exaggerated by linguistic and cultural differences.

The examination of the social implications of second homes in Wales has gone little further than this. It has already been stated that these examinations have been inadequate, and it is to the continuing interest in the sociological implications of second homes that the present study is addressed. Both the Wye College report and the D.A.R.T. survey outline certain areas where gaps in knowledge exist. The latter emphasizes the need for a further thinking through of the implications of second-home growth to one million or more, involving a more detailed analysis of the sociology of second homes. The Caernarfonshire survey expresses surprise that the social costs and benefits associated with the growth in numbers of second homes have not attracted the kind of empirical case study so frequently used to investigate the impact of commuters near cities.

The need exists for an objective and empirical study of the attitudes of the local inhabitants in receiving areas and an assessment of the impact of second-home ownership on local communities, as well as to assess the degree and extent of antagonism and to investigate how far such attitudes represent only minority views. In the next chapter the particular local factors which influenced the design of the present research are discussed, together with an examination of the particular local context of second-home ownership in the areas studied.

REFERENCES

(1) Downing, P. and Dower, M. (1973). *Second Homes in England and Wales*, Dartington Amenity Research Trust, Publication Number 7.

(2) Audits of Great Britain Limited (Annual). *Statistics on Second Dwellings* prepared for the Government Social Survey as at 31st March, 1968–72 inclusive.

(3) Bielckus, C. L., Rogers, A. W. and Wibberley, G. P. (1972). *Second Homes in England and Wales: a study of the distribution and use of rural properties taken over as second residences.* Countryside Planning Unit, Wye College.

(4) Pyne, C. B. (1972). *Second Homes*, Caernarfonshire County Planning Department.

(5) Jacobs, C. A. J. (1972). *Second Homes in Denbighshire*, Research Report Number 3, Denbighshire County Planning Office (January 1972).

(6) Tuck, C. J. (1973). *Second Homes*, Merioneth Structure Plan Subject Report Number 17, Merioneth County Planning Office.

(7) de Vane, R. (1975). *Second-Home Ownership, a case study*, University of Wales Press, Cardiff.

(8) Carr, J. P. and Morrison, W. I. (1972). *A Survey of Second Homes in East Monmouthshire*, Monmouthshire Studies Report Number 7: Planning Research Group, Enfield College of Technology (Middlesex Polytechnic).

(9) Archer, B. (1973). *The Impact of Domestic Tourism*, University of Wales Press, 1973.

(10) Liverpool University Department of Civic Design (1973). *Second Homes in North Wales.*

(11) Downing, P. and Dower, M. op. cit., p. 30.

FURTHER READING

(1) Welsh Council (1974). *Housing in Wales*, Chapter 7, Welsh Office, Cardiff.

(2) Cwmni Gwasg Rydd Caerdydd (1972). *Holiday Homes*, Report Number 3.

CHAPTER 2

A GENERAL DESCRIPTION OF THE SURVEY

It has been pointed out that previous research into second homes at both the national and local level has indicated certain areas where knowledge is inadequate, basically that little work has been carried out to assess accurately the sociological impact of second-home ownership in receiving areas. Within North Wales intra-regional and intra-county differences can readily be illustrated. To explain the main lines research was to follow and the considerations which guided its design it is helpful to look briefly at local authority attitudes[1] towards second homes within the old counties of North Wales for which information is available. The intra-regional differences and the local debates for and against second homes were important in defining our field of study.

Within the old county of Caernarfonshire the Lleyn Peninsula is the area most densely populated by second homes and Dwyfor District Council feel that this is causing concern throughout the area. Replying to the interim Caernarfon-shire County Council Second-Homes Report, the old Lleyn Rural District Council[2] maintained that it obscured the real issue of second homes, namely 'The widespread and active competition for existing dwellings from outside, against the residents of this and other districts who with a low income are unable to compete in an active and lucrative market, which derives its impetus to a very large extent from the sponsorship given by the Government, unintentionally perhaps, to the making of money available towards renovating second homes'. The Council argued that people were being forced to leave Lleyn because of the 'unhealthy economic background created by weak housing legislation'[3] and to this extent the Lleyn Council illegally withheld standard grants as well as dis-cretionary improvement grants to non-residents. The new Dwyfor Council feel that the costs of ownership far outweigh the benefits – the Welsh way of life which manifests itself, for example, in local eisteddfodau will inevitably suffer from an influx of non-Welsh-speaking people. They argue that there should be no more development in Dwyfor and that another of the old county's districts, Arfon to the south and east, would be better able to cope with such an influx because of its large number of derelict quarry buildings.

Arfon Borough Council feel similarly that second homes contribute to the dilution of the Welsh way of life, but argue that permanent non-Welsh residents have an even worse effect on the language. As far as the slate valleys of the Borough accepting second-home owners is concerned, the Council argue that these areas still have an essentially Welsh culture which should be preserved. Aberconwy

District Council to the east feel that in some areas the only alternative to second homes is the dereliction of properties, but it preferred that small industries should be encouraged in such areas to retain native communities.

Meirionydd District Council feel that the situation is worse in the old county of Merioneth even than in Caernarfon, and that although it is difficult to produce statistical evidence of the dilution of Welsh culture, this must inevitably result from an influx of persons with a different language and culture. The decline in culture and services is more of a problem in remote rural areas than on the coast. The Denbighshire[4] report sees a second home density of 12% of the housing stock as the present saturation level for its parishes, and the possible threshold level after which social problems become more serious.

In their draft Structure Plan Gwynedd County Council feel that although it is impossible to identify precise criteria which define an acceptable level of second-home ownership, as this depends on matters such as the development patterns and the attitudes of local people which are difficult to measure, in those areas where growth is causing concern new housing development should be limited to providing for the needs of local people. The Council identifies the two types of area in the county most affected by second homes, namely small villages and hamlets in tourist areas where local housing demand is small and where once a significant proportion of houses are second homes the community sense disappears, and larger villages in similar areas where there is a local demand for housing. There exists the need to exercise a degree of control over a situation which in their opinion was getting out of hand and affecting communities detrimentally. This was consistent with their aim to preserve the unique identity of the area and to create favourable conditions for preserving and developing the Welsh language and culture.

From this background to the situation within North Wales, the types of questions which should be investigated and the types of area where investigation should be carried out began to suggest themselves. The main issues which needed to be examined were the attitudes of people affected by second-home development and the degrees of interaction between second-home owners and native people in the areas which have received them. These issues could be related to the density and location of second homes within the receiving areas and the examination could serve the dual purpose of assessing the degree to which some local authority views are correct as well as attempting to provide some criteria by which the effects of second homes on receiving areas could be measured. Further, certain types of areas suggested themselves, namely the Lleyn Peninsula, the inland quarrying areas, the Merioneth uplands, and an area where second homes still comprised only a small proportion of the local housing stock. Within these areas villages could be selected and examined in relation to the sometimes emotional assertions based frequently on inadequate knowledge which have to some extent become a feature of the second-home debate, particularly in Wales.

Having regard to this and within the temporal and financial constraints of the research programme, four study areas were chosen:

Penmachno and Cwm Penmachno

Both settlements are areas of high density second homes in a rural context, and second homes are to be found in quantity both in the main settlements and in the surrounding area.

Situated in the Machno Valley, the upper reaches of the Conwy Valley, Penmachno and Cwm Penmachno were originally mining and quarrying villages. The Cwm is situated some $2\frac{1}{2}$ miles up the valley from Penmachno and until the early 1960s buses used to take workers daily to the quarries at Cwm. At one time there were five quarries working but the last was closed in 1972. Both settlements could be described as ribbon in form, the housing in Cwm primarily comprising rows of terraced cottages whilst in Penmachno the type of housing is more variable with a number of small cottages and larger farmhouses to be found on the valley sides and in the valley itself. Penmachno is serviced by three shops, a post office, two hotels and a small petrol service station, and possesses an infants' school and a small council estate. Public transport is limited but three or four buses run on weekdays to and from Llanrwst.

Rhiw

A coastal area of high density second-home ownership with a fairly scattered distribution, Rhiw is situated on the Lleyn Peninsula in what is basically a cattle farming area, and is bounded on the east by Porth Neigwl. Mynydd y Rhiw has possessed a manganese mine which was closed after the First World War, reopened during the Second and then closed again. Fishing for crayfish and lobsters has declined in the last few decades. The housing is scattered, evidence of the high numbers of small holdings which historically characterized the area. The village is serviced by a post office and garage but public transport is non-existent, the nearest bus route ending at Aberdaron some $3\frac{1}{2}$ miles away. A certain amount of land in the area is owned by the National Trust.

Croesor

An inland area exhibiting medium density second-home ownership. The village itself is sited about 500 feet above sea level and at a distance of about five miles as the crow flies from the sea and Porthmadog. Croesor is to be found near the top of the Croesor Valley of about half a mile in extent, bounded on one side by the mountain range terminating in Cnicht (2,250 ft.) and on the other by the Moelwyn which at its peak is 100 feet higher. The settlement originally served to house the men who worked further up the valley at Croesor (Moelwyn Mawr) and Park Slate Quarries, both of which closed early in the 1930s. The village is very isolated. It is not served by public transport and there is no main road within three miles. It is served by a school and a post office which is not a general store, but the nearest public house is some 45 minutes walk away.

Llansannan

A rural inland area exhibiting a low density, scattered second-home ownership, Llansannan is primarily an agricultural area situated in the Denbigh uplands on the main Denbigh to Llanrwst road. Development has been in ribbon form although the settlement does possess a small council estate, and a feature of the village is the new housing which is to be found on the Denbigh road out of the village. Llansannan is served by two shops, a post office with a small petrol station, two public houses and a school. Public transport is fairly regular with some six buses a day to and from Denbigh and Rhyl. A mile or so away is the small settlement of Tan-y-fron which comprises a few scattered houses and a small council estate.

Within these four areas the first task was to prepare a preliminary list of potential second-home owners. In the first instance this was carried out by reference to the rating registers of the district councils which serve the respective areas. As previous research has pointed out, these alone are an inadequate statistical base as the degree of accordance of away addresses for demand notes and actual second homes can vary to some extent with the whim of the second-home owner. Thus evidence obtained from the rating registers was complemented by reference to the relevant electoral registers and the supplementary help and knowledge of local people. It was felt that this combination of sources would give a reasonably accurate picture of the numbers and locations of second homes within the study areas although as visits to the areas became more frequent during the actual fieldwork it became clearer that some minor alterations to the lists were necessary. The preliminary lists were used as sample frames during the fieldwork.

The project was divided into two main stages:

Postal Survey

A questionnaire was designed to be sent to the first home address of all second-home owners identified in the preliminary lists. The aim was to obtain information concerning the use of second homes, the reasons for their acquisition, the links if any of their owners with Wales, and the general socio-economic background to second-home ownership in the four study areas. Many of the questions in the questionnaire were similar to those which had been asked by Caernarfonshire, Merioneth and Denbighshire County Planning Departments in their surveys of second homes in the area and it was felt that because of this it could reasonably be assumed that problems of design, layout and question wording would be minimized. Consequently little pilot work was undertaken and the questionnaire was posted to the first homes of second-home owners in March 1975 together with a stamped addressed envelope and a request for its return not later than the middle of April. If needed, three reminders were sent to the owners, and by mid-May it was felt that all questionnaires that were going to be returned had indeed been received.

At the outset it was realized that a study of this nature might arise some strong feelings both because it was an investigation into the private affairs of second-home owners and because of the emotions and feelings which the issue of second homes had raised, particularly in Wales. Not surprisingly the postal survey did arouse comment, but adverse replies made up only a small proportion of the response and there were more replies expressing interest and support for the project. At the end of the postal questionnaire, respondents were provided with a sheet of paper on which they were invited to record some of their feelings towards and experiences of second-home own rship in North Wales and this provided some interesting and informative insights into their relationships with the respective study areas.

The Personal Interview Survey

The second stage of investigation involved the personal interviewing of samples of both local residents and second-home owners in the study areas. Question-naires, fairly similar in nature, were designed for both, their main aims being:

    (1)   To assess the relationships of the local residents and the second-home owners with the particular study area and with its existing institutions, and their beliefs and feelings toward the area.

    (2)   To assess the relationships between local residents and second-home owners.

    (3)   To measure the prevalent attitudes of the people affected by second-home development in the study areas.

Probability samples of the over-18 resident population were selected from the electoral registers of the respective study areas, ranging from 10% in those areas with the largest resident population to 25% where this is much smaller. Interviews with local people were almost exclusively carried out through the medium of the

Welsh language. Probability samples of second-home owners in the study areas were also selected, but here problems of non-response were acute. The twin difficulties of locating and then securing the response of owners were the main causes of this. It is possible that second-home owners have begun to tire from what has recently been an upsurge of interest in them; perhaps they have been over-surveyed. However, discussion with local residents indicated that many owners did not use their properties as often, perhaps, as has been suggested by previous research. The response of second-home owners to the personal interview survey has been disappointingly low and this has necessitated a correspondingly greater reliance upon information received from the local residents. Interviewing both with local residents and second-home owners was carried out in August and September 1975. An important consideration throughout the development of the research was the formulation of hypotheses concerning such factors as the density, location and type of second homes. If in the longer term real incomes rise, with increasing demands for recreational and leisure pursuits, the numbers and proportions of second homes in the United Kingdom, much lower than in most other developed countries, can be expected to increase. In this case it is important to know under what circumstances the social costs of ownership outweigh the economic benefits of receiving areas. Without negotiating the complexities of a fully-fledged cost-benefit analysis, if such factors as the density, location, type and use of second homes can be quantified it is important to under-stand the effects that they have on native settlements and communities. The aim has been to look at the possibility of quantifying more precisely the variables in such imprecise terms as 'excessive social costs' and 'maximum levels judged to be acceptable' which are to be found in some of the previous works of second homes. At the local level this, it was hoped, could both shed some light on local authority problems of developing a policy towards second-home development in North Wales, and help to find what could be called the 'tolerable limits' of second-home ownership, before second homes become perhaps unwitting agents of social disruption and the communal and political hostility this can provoke.

At the outset and in the light of previous research it was felt that relationships would exist between the attitudes of native people and the density and location of second homes in their areas. Underlying this would be the degree to which second-home owners interact with local people, the extent to which they involve themselves in local activities, and whether or not they become integrated into the local community. This in turn may be linked to the way in which the density and location of second homes in a particular area has led to the disintegration of what may be called the 'community feeling' and the 'Welsh way of life'. Consequently the aim was to look at the impact of second-home ownership on traditional

14

institutions and the discernible consequences for interaction between local people and newcomers in the four study areas.

REFERENCES

(1) Much of this discussion, except where specific reference is otherwise made, is taken from the transcripts of the second-homes debate in the public inquiry into the *Gwynedd Structure Plan*, held in early summer, 1975.

(2) PYNE, C. B.op cit. , p. 60.

(3) IBID, p. 63.

(4) JACOBS, C. A. J. op. cit.

CHAPTER 3

THE POSTAL QUESTIONNAIRE

The intention in this Chapter is to examine the results of the postal questionnaire which was sent to all the owners of second homes identified in the four study areas. This survey was designed to elicit information concerning the use of second homes, the reasons for their acquisition, the links of their owners with Wales and the socio-economics of second-home ownership particular to the four areas studied. Whilst all the surveys which have been carried out by County Planning Departments in North Wales have collected similar data for their counties as a whole it was necessary to undertake a preliminary study of this kind both to understand more fully the statistical background to ownership in the four areas and to gauge some of the factors that would be involved in the personal interviewing which was to follow. First of all, however, it is necessary to examine the four study areas and their densities and location of second homes in more detail.

Table 2

Second Homes and Response Rates in the Five Villages

	Pen-machno	Cwm Pen-machno	Croesor	Rhiw	Llan-sannan
Number of properties	222	108	36	55	248
Number of second homes	52	56	12	29	22
Density of second homes	23.4%	51.8%	33.3%	52.7%	8.9%
Number of responses	28	28	5	17	16
Response rate	53.8%	50.0%	41.7%	58.6%	72.7%

The table presents the number of properties identified in each of the study areas, the number identified as second homes, and the proportion this represents of the total. It will be seen that the density of second homes as a percentage of the housing stock is highest in Rhiw, 52.7%, and lowest in Llansannan, 8.8%. When the figures for Penmachno and Cwm Penmachno are combined, an overall density of second-home ownership of 32% is found, but relative to the housing stock the larger proportion of second homes is to be found in the Cwm. It should also be noted that of the 171 second homes identified in the sample areas over 63% are to be found in the Penmachno area. The table also indicates the response rates which were achieved to the postal questionnaire, which ranged from a disappointing 42% in Croesor to an encouraging 73% in Llansannan.

Overall the response rates were slightly better than might have been expected considering the upsurge of interest which has been shown in second-home owners by researchers at many levels.

Certain clear patterns emerged concerning the location of second homes in the study areas. In Penmachno and Cwm the large majority of second homes are to be found in the centre of the settlements and along the B4406 (Cwm road) which joins the two settlements. This is a direct result of properties which used to house quarry workers coming up for sale as the industry declined. The percentage of all second homes in the two areas so situated is between 80–85%, the remainder being located lower down the valley near Penmachno itself as the valley widens. A similar central pattern is to be found in Croesor, where a number of second homes are again to be found in the terraces of the main settlement, with fewer to be found along the valley side. Rhiw and Llansannan exhibit an altogether different pattern. In Llansannan the second homes are scattered and very much isolated from the main settlement, and are often only to be reached via dirt roads. In Rhiw the second homes are less scattered, with a small proportion to be found at or near the crossroads at Mynydd yr Rhiw, but most are scattered around the Mynydd, several with attractive and sweeping views of Porth Neigwl.

A significant problem which had to be overcome was that concerning the criteria by which each of our four study areas were defined. In the cases of Penmachno and Cwm, and Croesor, criteria were easy to determine. In the former cases the decision was made according to the situation of a property within the Machno Valley and because of the mainly centralized location of second homes in the area this was a fairly simple exercise. This was also true in Croesor where the actual criterion used was whether or not the property concerned fell within the catchment area of the village school, a boundary which corresponds well to the physical boundaries which separate Croesor from other small settlements within Llanfrothen parish. However, in Llansannan parish and in Rhiw, which is a scattered settlement with an ill-defined physical boundary, it was necessary to establish criteria by which a property could be regarded as within the settlement *per se*. After detailed fieldwork in these two areas, properties in the main cluster of houses in Rhiw and on the Mynydd, together with properties within the electoral ward of Llansannan excluding Bylchau, Llanfair Talhaiarn and Rhiw Groes, where there are few if any second homes, were determined to be appropriate for our purposes. The figures presented in Table 2 refer to these definitions of our study areas.

The following sections present some descriptions concerning second-home ownership in the survey areas. The figures for Croesor should be treated with caution throughout, because of the low numbers involved, but most figures are presented as percentages for convenience.

Properties used as second homes

No newly or purpose built properties were identified as second homes by the postal survey in any of the study areas, all the properties being either old or modernized on their acquisition. This is indicative of the type of property which is used as a second home in these areas; the majority in all cases were in need of modernization on purchase. Observation in the field revealed that this was also true about those second homes whose owners did not reply to the questionnaire, and this obviated the difficulties which could have been faced concerning a definition of second homes which included chalets and caravans.

Tenure of properties

Over 85% of second homes in all the study areas except Croesor are owned freehold by their owners. In Croesor many second homes, and indeed many natively owned properties, are owned by Parc estate from which they are either leased or rented. The Afon Croesor effectively divides the village into that area where houses are owned by their occupiers, and that where they are leased and rented. The majority of second homes in the samples from Rhiw and Llansannan were acquired over ten years ago whilst in Penmachno and Cwm Penmachno the figure is between 40–50%. In Croesor the majority acquired their second home between 5–10 years ago, but this conclusion must be treated with caution because of the low numbers involved, and conversations with local residents revealed that several of the second homes have been occupied as such for considerably longer than ten years.

Acquisition of the properties

The most interesting feature which emerged here was the large proportion of owners who first found out that their property was vacant from friends and relatives. This could be indicative of the formation of 'colonies' of second-home owners in particular areas. We were not able to investigate this possibility at this stage, but with a considerable proportion of second homers owning first homes in the North West of England it is possible that areas have been subjected to groups of friends, or at least people known to each other, purchasing houses together. A fair proportion of owners found out that their properties were for sale by passing by and inquiring, and in general answers to this question indicate that a fairly sizeable proportion of second homers have previous links with North Wales, if only by way of a limited number of previous visits.

Previous occupiers of properties

Penmachno, Cwm Penmachno and Llansannan all exhibit an even split between present second homes which were previously occupied by a local person employed in the area and those which were occupied by previous second-home owners. In Rhiw the proportion of properties that were previously occupied by a local person employed in the area is much higher. It is possible that the effective closure of the slate quarries in Penmachno and Cwm which dates from the late 1950s and early 1960s was more advanced than the migration from Rhiw which caused properties to come on the market, and that a larger proportion and certainly a larger number of properties in Penmachno had been bought up by earlier second-home owners who subsequently sold up and moved from the area. In all areas except Penmachno nearly all second-home owners who have owned a second home for over ten years had acquired it from a local person employed in the area. However, since no data were collected concerning the number of owners of a property since it was last occupied by a native person it is not possible to resolve this issue satisfactorily.

Of those properties previously occupied by a local person 50% in both Llansannan and Rhiw first came to the notice of the present owners by way of relatives and friends. This figure, at between 25–30%, is much lower in Cwm and Penmachno. Slightly more owners acquired their properties from a local person if they had previous family links with Wales. However, there is no relationship between the category of previous owner and the present owner's ability to speak the Welsh language. If the property was last occupied by a second-home owner rather than by a local person it was more likely to have been a modernized old property on its acquisition by the present owner. It is possible that a certain amount of time had elapsed between the vacation of the property by a local person and its acquisition by a second-home owner, and also possible that the standards expected by a second-home owner were higher than those accepted by the previous occupant.

Table 3

Second Homes: Bedroom and Visitor Group Size

	Pen-machno	Cwm Pen-machno	Croesor	Rhiw	Llan-sannan
Average no. of bedrooms	2.392	2.392	3.000	2.647	2.250
Average size visitor group	4.142	4.035	3.400	5.058	4.000
Average no. of persons per bedroom	1.731	1.686	1.133	1.911	1.777

Table 3 indicates the average number of bedrooms in the second homes in the study areas. The figure for Croesor must again be treated with caution because of the low numbers in the sample. The average number of bedrooms is slightly higher in Rhiw than in the other areas. This is linked to the average size of the visitor group which, with the exception of Croesor, increases with the average number of bedrooms in the property, and implies an average bedroom occupancy of just under two.

Table 4

Reasons for the Acquisition of Second Homes in North Wales

Reason for acquisition	Pen-machno	Cwm Pen machno	Croesor	Rhiw	Llan-sannan
Mountain scenery	21	27	20	22	20
Coastal scenery	5	14	5	26	6
Nearness to home	8	11	0	6	13
Links with the area	16	14	17	15	15
Price of property	6	10	0	4	10
Other natural factors	12	6	4	1	6
Social reasons	3	1	7	0	2
Other economic reasons	0	1	0	2	2
No answer	29	16	47	24	26
	100	100	100	100	100

NOTE: This weighted average of the reasons for the acquisition of the property is found from:

$$\frac{}{r} = 100 \frac{\Sigma pi\ ri}{p\Sigma ri}$$ where   p = number of people in sample
ri = rth reason in the ith position
pi = the number of people choosing the rth reason in the ith position.

Local arrangements

At least half of all owners in all areas except Croesor claim to have an arrangement with a local person to clean or look after their second home. The existence of such an arrangement does not seem to be related to the links the second-home owner has with Wales or to his or her ability to speak Welsh, and as such, although it could provide a link with the local community for the second-home owner, it should probably be seen as an informal and limited arrangement. There is a tendency for second-home owners living furthest away from their second home to be more likely to have such an arrangement. Although there is little indication that they spend less time in their second homes than other owners living nearer, it is possible that their visits are less frequent. No significant relationship exists between the length of time a second-home owner has owned his or her property and the likelihood that he or she will have an arrangement with a local person.

Reasons for the acquisition of properties in North Wales

Respondents were asked to choose any five reasons for their choice of North Wales as the location of their second home, and to rank these in order of import-ance. We can obtain a weighted average for the importance of the reasons which influenced this choice, as shown in Table 4, and while this is not statistically sophisticated it enables us to see clearly the relative average importance of the reasons which influenced the choice of North Wales. Consistent similarities can be seen in all study areas for the rankings of scenery and family or sentimental ties with the area. Apart from the obvious scenic attractions of North Wales, a clearly important factor in choice would seem to have been people's previous links and associations with the area. This may be an important consideration in second-home owners' attitudes towards local people and local institutions, and consequently in local people's reactions towards second-home owners. We can go on to examine the types of links with Wales that are claimed by the second-home owner.

Two-fifths of the second-home owners in our samples of Penmachno, Cwm Penmachno and Croesor claim to have had no previous links with Wales, and this figure rises to 53% and 56% respectively in Rhiw and Llansannan. Of those who have links with Wales these mainly concern birthplace or relatives in the principality. It seemed that second-home owners with surnames such as Williams or Jones, names which aroused a certain amount of curiosity on our part as to their family links with Wales, were often third, fourth or even fifth generation descend-ants of people actually born in Wales. A fairly large proportion of respondents, between 35–40% in all areas, claim to be able to speak or to be learning Welsh, but a similar proportion of second homers are not interested in learning the language at all.

Leisure activities

Respondents were asked to identify their main leisure activities while at their second homes. These revealed very few surprises in any study area. Outdoor recreation was clearly the most popular activity, ranging from mountain walking in Snowdonia to sailing off the Lleyn Peninsula, followed by resting and touring North Wales by car. A small proportion of owners listed making house repairs as a leisure activity which perhaps reinforces the view of the second-home owner

21

as taking pride in his 'home from home'. Apart from these active pursuits, other activities included rounds of entertaining, resting, and other indoor activities such as reading, writing and painting.

A socio-economic profile of ownership

Table 5

A Socio-Economic Profile of Second-Home Owners

	Penmachno	Cwm Penmachno	Croesor	Rhiw	Llansannan
A/B	32%	18%	100%	65%	50%
C1	54%	50%	—	35%	50%
C2	14%	25%	—	—	—
DIE	—	—	—	—	—
No answer	—	7%	—	—	—
N =	28	28	5	17	16

Table 5 indicates the socio-economic group of second-home owners in the study areas. Several points of interest are apparent. Firstly the fairly high numbers of skilled working-class people owning a second home in Penmachno and Cwm. This seems to be far removed from the popular view of second homers as members of the higher professional classes of society, and consequently of a higher socio-economic grouping than the native residents of the community to which they have come. The people in category C2 had in nearly all cases owned their homes in Penmachno and Cwm for over ten years, and this, combined with the fact of the low price of property in the old slate quarrying areas at this time, can explain to some extent this rather surprising finding. Although no data were collected concerning house prices at the time of purchase, it became clear through conversations both with second-home owners and with local residents that house prices at the time of the quarry closures were exceptionally low, and in any case were never particularly high for some of the terraced properties in Penmachno and Cwm. In only one case was the second home found to be a joint purchase with another family and in no case was the second home rented. The lower price of property at the time of acquisition must have been one important factor in the decision to purchase.

There is a significant number of second-home owners from socio-economic group C1 in all areas except Croesor. Many of these were teachers or others similarly placed in the lower professional groups able to take advantage of the longer holidays available to them. Still a high proportion of owners in Croesor and Rhiw, and to a lesser extent, Llansannan, are from the higher professional groups A and B. This is often expected to be the case because of the higher incomes and mobility associated with members of such socio-economic groups. In Rhiw and Llansannan the properties which are typical of second homes are more of the old farm or agricultural dwelling type, as opposed to the old quarryman's terraced house in Penmachno and Cwm, and are quite likely to have commanded a higher purchase price, a supposition again borne out by conversations in the field.

In all areas except Croesor most second-home owners were employed rather than self-employed. However, the self-employed were well represented in our sample and this is only to be expected for such people are both able to distribute their time in such a way as to derive maximum benefit from ownership and are quite likely to be found in the higher income brackets. What is much more surprising is the three owners in Llansannan and the one rentee in Penmachno who are unemployed.

Income

Data were collected concerning the total family income of second homers, both at present and at the time the second home was acquired. At the time of acquisition a significant proportion of people in Cwm Penmachno were earning less than £1,000 p.a., and over a half of the respondents had a family income of under £1,500 p.a. Again this may be indicative of the lower price of property in the old slate quarrying areas. Proportionately a significantly higher number of second-home owners were in the higher income brackets at the time of purchase. It is likely that many of those in the lower income brackets purchased their homes quite early in life. Second-home owners' incomes at the time of response were considerably higher on average in all study areas than the average adult male workers' earnings in all industries for October 1974. The percentage of owners with family incomes exceeding £4,000 p.a. at the time of response ranges from 35% and 45% in Cwm and Penmachno to 50% and 54% in Rhiw and Llansannan. The higher figure for Llansannan may be related to the lower proportion of second homers who are retired.

Marital status

As might be expected the large majority of second homers in all areas were married. The highest proportion of owners who are single, widowed or divorced is to be found in Rhiw.

Education

The percentage of owners possessing a degree or other higher education qualification varies from 36% in Cwm to 38% and 39% respectively in Llansannan and Penmachno, and 59% in Rhiw. The proportions in Cwm and Penmachno of owners leaving school between the ages of 0–15 probably correspond to the 'self-made men' and the relatively high proportion of blue-collar workers with second homes in these areas. Again it is possible that those who left school at the intermediate stage between the ages of 15–20 years correspond with socio-economic group C1.

First-home location of owners

The conurbations of England are clearly found to be the major exporters of second-home owners to the study areas, with the nearest conurbation, the North West of England, providing over 60% of the owners in Llansannan, Penmachno and Cwm. The G.L.C. area and the Home Counties provide nearly one-third of the second-home owners in Rhiw, which may be related to the higher prices of property in that area and the consequent lesser importance of travel costs to those able to own a second property in this most isolated of our study areas. Although not statistically significant the data indicated that those owners with first homes in areas furthest away from North Wales had acquired their second homes at an earlier date than those from the nearer conurbations. A comparison of our responses with the complete lists of second-home owners reveals that no major exporting region of second-home owners was seriously under-represented.

Retirement

In Penmachno and Llansannan a majority of owners said that they definitely intended to retire to their second homes. In all areas socio-economic groups A and B contained a slightly higher proportion of those who were definitely intending to retire to their second homes, and this positive decision was well spread over all the regions of first home origin. However, no particular relationship was found in any of the areas between the decision to retire and either the links of owners with Wales or their ability to speak or interest in the Welsh language. Retirement represents an important change of use of the second home and the positive decision to retire may be indicative of the second-home owners' assessment of the degree to which they have been accepted into the local community and the likelihood that their retirement years will be spent happily in a house and a community that once they only visited on average for less than a quarter of a year.

Occupancy rates

Table 6 indicates the average number of days per month that the second home is occupied and the percentage of this time which is accounted for by persons other than the family group of the owner or rentee. In Llansannan only one owner admitted to letting or hiring out his home, but it was not occupied by other than the family during the year concerned. The area with the highest proportion of second homes let out was Penmachno where nearly one-third of owners said that they hired out their properties. Consequently, apart from Croesor, where the figures must once again be treated with caution because of the low number of respondents, it is in Penmachno that second homes are occupied on average for the most days each year. In all cases occupancy rates exhibit the expected summer peaking and in all areas except Cwm Penmachno a fortnight at least was spent in the second homes in August.

Clearly occupancy is another factor which can be important in determining the relationship of the second home owner with the receiving community. It is unlikely that short term lettees of second homes as holiday accommodation will make such an impact on the receiving areas as the owners who make regular visits to their homes, but families who occupy their second homes on average for upwards of a quarter of a year can be expected to have a continuing impact on the villages which receive them.

Respondents were provided with space to make any comments they wished concerning second-home ownership in general and their experiences of ownership in particular. The majority of respondents did so. Comments from all study areas included particulars concerning the circumstances surrounding the acquisition of the property and details of its structure, position and the improvements which it had subsequently undergone. Certainly large numbers of respondents expressed the enjoyment they had obtained from their experiences of ownership and their pleasure at the way they had been received by local residents. Several respondents explained that at the time they had purchased their properties the question of second-home ownership was not a contentious issue and that in their opinion it had become so only in very recent years. Many pointed to the particular economic circumstances which had led to their property being on the market and felt that it was indeed late now to accuse them of being a cause of the emigration which has to a greater or lesser extent affected all our study areas. A number of respondents listed complaints which they felt had reduced their enjoyment of second-home ownership, such as 'extortionate' water rates and the attitudes of local planning authorities to proposed alterations' in their property. A small minority regarded the questionnaire as 'impertinent and felt that it did not take account of the friendships they had made in the area and the way they had mixed

Table 6

Second-Home Owners' Occupancy Rates

Month	Penmachno		Cwm Penmachno		Croesor		Rhiw		Llansannan	
	Occupancy days	% non-family	Occupancy days	% non-family	Occupancy days	% non-family	Occupancy days	% non-family	Occupancy days	% non-family
March	4.535	11.0	5.428	8.5	16.400	36.5	3.117	0.0	6.312	0.0
April	8.749	12.2	6.356	8.4	13.000	21.5	10.352	13.6	8.875	0.0
May	9.213	15.1	6.320	2.2	10.400	26.9	7.352	11.1	7.812	0.0
June	10.892	19.9	9.106	14.1	13.400	44.7	11.293	7.2	12.500	0.0
July	15.535	24.5	10.571	5.4	6.000	0.0	13.941	16.8	13.937	0.0
August	19.356	18.2	12.963	12.1	16.200	17.2	17.882	14.4	17.437	0.0
September	11.713	12.1	8.142	14.0	18.800	4.2	12.294	13.3	7.000	0.0
October	8.499	19.3	6.356	8.4	12.800	0.0	4.823	17.0	6.687	0.0
November/December	3.678	23.7	2.535	0.0	8.400	0.0	1.852	22.1	2.531	0.0
January/February	2.892	21.6	2.500	0.0	9.600	0.0	1.705	27.5	3.250	0.0
Total	95.062	17.9	70.277	8.8	125.000	16.9	84.611	13.4	86.341	0.0

with local people and felt part of the community.

The following section presents some selections from the comments that were received. As far as is possible they represent a cross-section of the opinions of second-home owners and their experiences. It would be wrong to attempt an interpretation of these opinions at this stage and possibly at any subsequent stage. However, in the following chapters when relationships and attitudes in the study areas are examined more fully, they will be put in the context of second-home owners' empirical relationships with, and the attitudes of, local people.

Penmachno

'We have experienced nothing but good relations to our family from all the local people and tradesmen. We have been attending Welsh language classes held in the village over the last six months and in this again we have received the utmost encouragement. Our relationship with other second-home owners in the village is also most friendly.'

'The political capital which has been made out of second homes in Wales I think is in many cases unfounded as many of the properties in our immediate area would have fallen down had not "foreigners" been willing to purchase.'

'Welsh people who strongly resent the presence of the "alien" English have the remedy in their own hands – they should sell their houses and cottages to their countrymen only.'

Cwm Penmachno

'We have several friends in the area. When we purchased the house in 1953, it cost £230.'

'We have received nothing but extreme kindness and friendship from the Welsh people living in the valley.'

'I made a great number of dear friends in Cwm Penmachno and was very sorry to see so many of them leaving to find work elsewhere – many years ago in the press it was called a dying village. I found the local people so helpful and friendly. I'm afraid it is a lot different with some of the newcomers – they seem to think they have bought the countryside as well as a cottage.'

'A second home in Wales is good for both sides – commercially for the Welsh and aesthetically for the English.'

'Some of us "foreigners" have over a period of years grown into the Welsh way of life, even to the extent of saying "Cymru am Byth".'

'We have been made extremely welcome by the indigenous folk. I think that much of the trouble one reads about second-home ownership in Wales stems from the ability of English people to try to dominate. I am English but when I go to Wales I recognize that I am their guest and they respond by being perfect hosts.'

'We are uncomfortably aware that ownership of a second home inflates house prices and changes the social composition and structure of the valley. However, the solution to the problem is an economic one and the labour market is more fundamental than the housing market.'

Croesor

'Over twenty years I dare to hope that I have made a few friends among my neighbours.'

'I have seen countless English people move to Wales with no real stake in the community . . . I think it is very difficult for an English person to be really part of the community.'

Rhiw

'Ownership has been a truly happy and rewarding experience. We have sensed no resentment on behalf of the Welsh folk living in and around Rhiw and on the contrary during the last ten years or so we have encountered friendliness and helpfulness on the part of all the local inhabitants.'

'The few local people remaining are all kindly and friendly towards us.'

'When an all-the-year-round resident moves out of his or her home into a caravan and lets their own home, are they classified as a second-home owner?'

Llansannan

'Contrary to popular myth I have not found the local people hostile to us having a second home in Wales.'

'Too many Welsh people are quick to condemn second-home owners as "usurpers of Welsh property and denying people homes". This feeling is particularly strong in my area . . . if there are cases where second-home purchasers have pushed up prices and Welsh people are suffering because of this then this is obviously wrong and something should be done about it. But not blanket legislation making life intolerable to all second-home owners.'

'We have formed firm friendships with many of the local Welsh people who are delighted with our interest in the Welsh language.'

'My wife and I respect the area for what it is. We sometimes feel a sense of resentment at some of the younger extreme nationalists, but this is understandable and to an extent acceptable.'

'Could we really visualize a situation where Wales was kept entirely for the Welsh?'

The picture which emerges from this look at the background of second-home ownership in our study areas confirms a number of the features found by the local authority studies which have taken place in North Wales, but it does possess some surprising features. The following points are worthy of note:

1. The basic differences between our study areas in terms of the density and location of second homes.
2. The large number of owners who claim to have various types of links with Wales.
3. The possibility of people known to each other settling in the study areas.
4. The fairly large proportion of owners who have arrangements with local people concerning their second homes, who expressed interest in the Welsh language and who are likely to retire to their second homes.
5. The perhaps surprisingly low socio-economic grouping of second-home owners in some areas.
6. The expected high occupancy rate of second homes, particularly in terms of that associated with other forms of holiday accommodation.
7. The high proportion who have owned their second home for upwards of ten years, and the numbers who bought them from previous second-home owners.
8. The considerable percentage of owners who are concerned with and have specific views on the current debate about second homes in Wales.

All these factors give rise to possible hypotheses concerning the relationships between second-home owners and local people and local organizations. The following chapters look at the interaction between local people and second-home owners and the attitudes of the former to the phenomenon of second-home ownership in their villages.

CHAPTER 4

THE PERSONAL INTERVIEW SURVEY – IMAGES OF SOCIETY

This Chapter primarily focuses upon local respondents' images of their localities, and upon their perceptions of social groupings in their environment. Towards the middle of the chapter the discussion focuses upon social imagery and the subjective perceptions of local people concerning the social stratification within their villages. It is hoped that this aspect of the study will form an important contribution to the debate concerning the influence of second homes and their owners on rural Wales, and some attempt is made in conclusion to link this with the relevant theory of class and status in rural villages. First of all, however, it is necessary to outline the samples of local residents and second-home owners which were interviewed in the study areas. Table 7 presents the relevant data for local residents.

Table 7
Local Residents Samples

	Penmachno		Cwm		Croesor		Rhiw		Llansannan	
	Male	Female	M.	F.	M.	F.	M.	F.	M.	F.
Number of Interviews	12	15	7	6	6	7	6	7	24	29
TOTAL	27		13		13		13		53	

The figures represent some 10% of the over-18 population in Penmachno, Cwm and Llansannan, rising to 25% in Croesor and Rhiw. The table shows the numbers of interviews carried out with men and women in the respective areas, although the sample was not stratified in this respect. Representative samples were selected from the electoral registers of the respective areas and those who wished, in fact the great majority, were interviewed through the medium of Welsh in August and September 1975. A very small number of people refused to participate in the survey. There were no refusals at all in Cwm Penmachno or Rhiw and, in all, refusals constituted less than 3% of all responses.

By contrast the response of second-home owners was most disappointing. In all, a total of only 24 owners were interviewed, 13 in Penmachno and Cwm, 5 in Rhiw, 4 in Llansannan and 2 in Croesor. The numbers concerned are so low as to make it impossible to establish a great deal about the second-home owner's point of view in terms of his or her attitudes towards the second-home area or in terms of the types of contacts made in the locality. The main reasons for this low response were the difficulties faced by interviewers in making contact with large numbers of owners and, when this was accomplished, in securing their participation in the study. Perhaps occupancy rates in August 1975 were lower than those suggested by the data for 1974 in the previous chapter, but in any case a greater reliance has had to be placed upon the interviews carried out with all-year-round residents, and the fact remains that in Croesor it was more difficult to elicit response from second-home owners in terms of participation both in the postal and in the personal interview survey.

The following paragraphs describe some basic characteristics of the resident population in the study areas, and consideration is given to their relationship with and length of residence in the respective localities. These data were elicited by a series of open-ended questions.

Only in Croesor were less than 45% of local respondents not actually born and brought up locally, but in all areas the percentage born and brought up in the old counties of North Wales, Anglesey, Caernarfon, Denbigh and Merioneth, exceeded 80%. Respondents not native to North Wales came primarily from the North West of England, the West Midlands, the London area and South Wales, but no pattern emerged as to whether they had previously been second-home owners in the villages concerned. There is a close linkage between the areas where respondents were born and those where they were brought up.

Table 8 indicates the average length of time that respondents had lived in their localities, together with the length of time they have lived at their present address.

Table 8

Local People's Length of Residence

	Years lived in village			Years lived at present address		
	Mean	Standard deviation	Coefficient of variability	Mean	Standard deviation	Coefficient of variability
Penmachno	36.04	22.57	0.63	22.67	20.36	0.90
Cwm	32.62	18.92	0.58	25.54	14.97	0.59
Croesor	22.31	18.37	0.82	16.15	12.33	0.76
Rhiw	41.70	20.23	0.49	28.69	16.64	0.58
Llansannan	25.17	18.58	0.74	18.40	18.99	1.03

NOTE: Coefficient of Variability $= \dfrac{\text{STANDARD DEVIATION}}{\text{MEAN}}$

The standard deviations relative to the mean show the expected wide deviations from the average, but the coefficient of variability aids a comparison between the areas in respect of the relative homogeneity of the length of time lived in the area with that lived at the present address, which is in turn an indication of internal mobility within the localities. Rhiw exhibits the longest average length of time lived in the village, together with the lowest concommitant coefficient of variability, which is indicative of the generally higher age level of respondents in the area. The only reversal of the general pattern of relationship between the average length of time lived in the area and at the present address is found between Penmachno and Cwm. The greater than unity coefficient of variability in the length of time spent by respondents at their present address is indicative of the wide range of answers received, but the general impression gained from all the villages is the relatively long history of many respondents' associations with the respective localities.

Relatively small percentages of respondents had lived outside Wales during their lifetimes, ranging from 15% in Penmachno, 23% in Cwm and Rhiw, to 25% in Llansannan and Croesor. A considerable proportion of these percentages refer in fact to respondents who were born and bred in England. Generally speaking the villages with the highest average length of residence had fewer respondents who had lived outside Wales. The main areas of residence outside the Principality were again the London area, the North West of England and the West Midlands, although no respondent in Penmachno or Rhiw had lived in more than one location outside Wales. Respondents were asked why they had come to live in the respective localities. Many had lived in the villages all their lives but the main reasons given by those who had not were employment and marriage. The Llansannan sample, which exhibited the highest proportion of English-born residents, contained nine respondents (17%) who said that they had come to live in the area for environmental reasons. These people may be similar to or even correspond to social elements 2 or 3, salaried immigrants and spiralists, described by Pahl in his work on the South East of England.[1]

The great majority of people in all the areas regarded their locality as their 'real home' rather than 'just as a place to live' and majorities in Croesor, Rhiw and Llansannan said that they had never seriously considered moving away. However, in Penmachno and Cwm majorities had given 'serious thought' to the possibility of leaving the village, and discussions revealed the two main reasons for this to be a lack of employment opportunities and the wish on behalf of older residents to live nearer friends and relatives. Often this would not have required a move out of the county but clearly it was not a move to be undertaken lightly.

'I'd like to leave here for a little while anyway. There are no opportunities in the area, but most of the people I know live here.'

26 years residence in Cwm.

'I'd never leave now I'm too old – where would I go? But most of my friends have gone.'

53 years residence in Penmachno.

The wish to follow one's friends or relatives in moving may be indicative of the more centralized location in Penmachno and Cwm of properties which are unoccupied for a large part of the year. Several elderly residents revealed in conversation that they sometimes felt isolated from help and assistance in times of need despite close associations with other local residents living nearby.

Respondents were asked what they would most miss about living in their localities if for some reason they had to leave them. The largest proportions in all areas felt that their friends were the most important aspects of life in their villages, and typical answers included:

'This is my area and I know everybody.'

Life residence in Llansannan.

'I love everything about the place, the people, the mountains, everything. This place is part of me.'

58 years residence in Penmachno.

'I'd never leave again – it was the biggest mistake I made. This is my home and my people, and I love it.'

46 years residence in Cwm.

'The close community spirit – it's like a family here.'

14 years residence in Croesor.

'The Welsh community and my friends and relations – but I'm too old to move anyway.'

Life residence in Rhiw.

Only in Llansannan was 'Welshness' specifically mentioned, indicating perhaps that the Welshness of an area is not thought of as distinct or separate from the people, but since the question did not specify where a respondent would move to, it is possible that the thought of moving away from Wales altogether may have elicited a somewhat different response. In Llansannan generally a wider variety of responses were found. Two respondents said that they would miss the chapel most of all if they had to leave, but the chapel of itself did not figure in answers from any other area. A notable feature of the Llansannan response was the tendency of English born and bred residents to consider such factors as the 'rural life' and the 'environment' *per se* as more important than the people of the area, again perhaps lending support to the view that they are more akin to the categories described by Pahl as social elements 2 or 3.

Nearly 50% of respondents in Penmachno and almost a third in Cwm said that they would in fact be quite prepared to leave their villages.

'I wouldn't mind leaving – the village has changed a great deal since I was a child.'

25 years residence in Cwm.

'It's a nice place but I'd like to go and live somewhere else. There's no work here and not much to do.'

19 years residence in Penmachno.

In both villages these responses were given by people who said that they had given serious thought to the possibility of leaving, but they were fewer in number and this leaves the probability again that a move from the area would not be undertaken lightly. It is noteworthy that a somewhat smaller percentage of respondents in Cwm and Rhiw, where second-home ownership density is highest, regarded other people living in the area as the most important part of their lives. This is perhaps related to the overall numbers of people living in the villages. One respondent in Rhiw remarked:

'I'd never leave now, I'm a part of the village. But it's not the same as when I was young. Many people have left and English people have come in their place. It's not the same.'

Over 70% of people in all the villages except Cwm Penmachno were positive in saying that they disliked nothing about their areas. In Cwm, however, a third of respondents said that they most disliked second homes.

'Yes, I think the invasion by second homes is deplorable – it's ruining the village life and killing the language.'

Seven years residence in Cwm.

A similar response was confined to Llansannan alone, where only one person mentioned second homes. The most frequently reported complaint from all areas concerned the remoteness of the villages. Whilst Penmachno, Cwm and Llansannan are served by public transport, and Croesor and Rhiw are not, the perception of remoteness is not confined merely to a lack of public transport. A small minority in Llansannan said that they most disliked Welsh nationalists:

'Welsh nationalists – most people in the village dislike them too.'

English born, ten years residence in Llansannan.

It was not clear what was meant to such respondents by the generic term 'Welsh nationalists' but the minority with such views were certainly not all English-born residents. The only other factors which were given mention in more than one area were an English-Welsh division (Penmachno, Croesor and Llansannan, but again by only a very small number of people), the lack of anything to do, a lack of entertainment (except Croesor), and the weather (in Penmachno,

Cwm and Llansannan). The complaint of an English-Welsh division was voiced by only four respondents in the whole survey (3.4% of all those interviewed) but it would be premature to put any interpretation on this until people's perceptions of group divisions in their localities are examined in greater detail.

Finally in this section we wanted to get some idea of local respondents' relationships with their neighbours, and the frequency of their contacts with them. Over three-quarters of respondents in all the villages said that they chatted with their neighbours frequently, and in spite of the fact that properties are generally more isolated in Llansannan and Rhiw than, for example, the terraced properties in Cwm, very little difference emerged between the areas in this respect. Over two-thirds of respondents in all areas again regarded their neighbours as 'friends' or 'close friends', and although respondents in Cwm and Rhiw were generally less likely to think that they would miss their friends in the village most of all if they had to leave the area, they regarded their neighbours as highly as they were regarded in the other villages. Frequency of contact with neighbours was also investigated. Over 80% of people interviewed in each of the villages had been in one of their neighbours' houses within a week of the date of interview, the highest percentage being found in Llansannan and the lowest in Rhiw. In all the villages more than a third of the people interviewed had visited their neighbours within the twenty-four hours previous to the interview, but Llansannan exhibited the lowest percentage in this category, possibly related to the physical distance between some of the outlying properties. The highest percentages in this category were found in Cwm and Croesor, areas with a high proportion of terraced housing. The highest percentages of respondents who thought that their neighbours were 'very friendly' were found in Panmachno and Cwm, but the percentages are really so high in all the villages as to make distinctions somewhat unnecessary.

The remainder of this chapter is concerned with local people's awareness of groups in their environment, which was examined both to find out whether a second-home owner/local people divide was apparent and to understand more fully other types of groupings within the localities concerned. We wanted to ascertain people's images of their villages in terms of their perceptions of lines of social exclusion, of social groupings, and of social class divisions and the criteria used in talking of class. These images will often be imprecise, but they can be shared by people of similar backgrounds in particular areas. It was felt that unprompted responses to open-ended questions would furnish better information in this respect, and at a time in the interview when no mention had been made of second homes nor of the purposes of the research in this context, respondents were asked whether they thought that social classes could be found in their villages.

Table 9 shows the responses to the question:

'People sometimes talk about social classes. Would you say that there are different classes to be found in Llansannan (Croesor) (Penmachno) Rhiw?'

Table 9

Perceptions of Social Class

Type of classes	Penmachno	Cwm	Croesor	Rhiw	Llansannan
I Middle class/					
Working class	3.7	0.0	15.4	15.4	5.7
II Intellectual/					
Ordinary people	3.7	0.0	0.0	0.0	0.0
III Professional/					
Ordinary people	3.7	0.0	15.4	0.0	1.9
IV Richer incomers /					
Native people	3.7	0.0	0.0	0.0	0.0
V Some English and Welsh people think they are superior	3.7	0.0	7.7	0.0	3.8
VI Chapel people/					
Other people	0.0	7.7	0.0	0.0	1.9
VII There are no classes	55.6	84.6	53.8	84.6	79.1
VIII Don't know	25.9	0.0	7.7	0.0	1.9
IX There are classes but don't know what they are	0.0	7.7	0.0	0.0	5.7

The first factor which became evident was that many people experienced some difficulty in understanding the question, and some were unable in this sense to use the vocabulary of class. Most interviews were carried out through the medium of Welsh in all the villages, but even where interviewers reverted to the English (the only terms in Welsh for upper, middle, working and lower classes are literal translations from the English) they were sometimes still met with incomprehension. Apart from this the table shows the large percentages who felt that social classes did not exist in their villages. Through discussion it became clear that some people who felt this way thought that classes could and did exist elsewhere – the concept of class was not irrelevant but neither were classes omnipresent. A small number of people felt that if classes did exist they would be more easily distinguished and understood by outsiders who had come to live in their areas, in some cases because of their closeness to and affinity with classes before they had moved in, and in others because of their lesser involvement in and knowledge of the local community. Interestingly the villages with the highest densities of second homes, Cwm Penmachno and Rhiw, did not differ noticeably in any of these respects from the others, and in fact the percentages who felt that social classes did not exist were slightly higher in Cwm and Rhiw. It may have been expected that in areas with high second-home ownership contact with people from outside, people with experience of social class and to some extent people bringing it with them, might have engendered a more clear-cut perception of social class divisions, but at this stage the evidence does not lend much support to this view.

Not all of those who did perceive of social classes in their villages articulated something akin to the sociologist's sense of class. Category V in the table would seem to be equating class with status pretention, again casting some doubt on the validity of the concept of class for respondents.

> 'Some people do think of themselves as superior, but not as much as
> in a town though.'
>
> Croesor.

Only in Cwm and Llansannan was mention made of membership of religious organizations as a source of class differences, but the frequency of response in any of the categories I to VI was rather low. Categories I to IV indicate something like the sociological sense of class, but only eight respondents in the whole survey (6%) mentioned class terms *per se*. Five respondents mentioned such attributes as 'intellectual' or 'professional', but only one in Penmachno, identified 'richer incomers' as a class distinct from the 'ordinary' local people. Four respondents felt that classes did exist but were unable or unwilling to define them.

The primary reason given for the absence of social classes was the homogeneous nature of the villages concerned. 77% of respondents in Rhiw, 46% in Cwm, 33% in Penmachno and Llansannan, and 31% in Croesor argued that their communities are unified and that there are no differences between their residents. This was often extended to cover what were variously described as 'the English', 'the incomers' and 'the new people'.

> 'No of course not. It's a small place and everyone pulls together.'
>
> Penmachno.
>
> 'Well I don't think there are any, not amongst the locals anyway. And
> the English seem to get on very well with each other, just as we get on
> with them.'
>
> Cwm.

'Everybody is the same here. It's a small place, not like a town where you would get such differences. The Welsh and English do mix.'

Rhiw.

'Everybody is similar here. The English have moved in but they are trying their best to mix.'

Llansannan.

'Everybody is similar. There are differences in income – wealthy farmers and others on social security, but no class differences.'

Croesor.

This last quotation is representative of the view of a number of people who were aware of differences in income and occupation in their villages, attributes important to the sociologist's definition of class, but felt that these did not imply the existence of social classes. In these cases the differences were not regarded as important to the balance of power and control in the villages and to this extent:

'Everybody pulls together here.'

Croesor.

'There doesn't seem to be any difference between anybody here. This is a democratic community.'

Llansannan.

A secondary and somewhat different reason given for the absence of social classes in all the villages except Croesor is illustrated by the following quotations:

'This is a small village and that sort of thing cannot make itself apparent here.'

Penmachno.

'This is just a typical village community – they can't afford to be class-conscious in such a small place.'

Llansannan.

Such respondents did not specifically argue the positive unity of the villages but felt they were too small to afford differences of class. Smaller numbers still emphasized the presence of linguistic and cultural differences between the English and the Welsh, but felt again that these were not manifested in class distinctions.

'There are differences, not class just language and culture.'

Penmachno.

30% of respondents in Penmachno, 23% in Llansannan and Croesor, and 15% in Cwm and Rhiw did not think that classes existed in their villages, but were unable or unwilling to say why this was the case.

What is important to an understanding of local people's perceptions of social class is the extent to which classes and class differences of the kind mentioned carry with them automatic divisive consequences for the villages concerned, and in this context it is interesting to examine whether respondents employ a vocabulary most approaching that of class, an economic category based on wealth, occupation, or property, or one of social status based on differences of prestige, education and life-styles. Local people were asked to list those factors which they thought to be important in determining a person's class, and Table 10 presents the responses to the question:

'What sort of things decide what class of person belongs to would you say?'

Table 10

Criteria of Class

Class criteria	Penmachno	Cwm	Croesor	Rhiw	Llansannan
Money	7.4	15.4	15.4	15.4	11.3
Occupation	3.7	0.0	0.0	15.4	3.8
Education	0.0	7.7	7.7	7.7	0.0
Where one comes from	0.0	0.0	7.7	0.0	0.0
Family background	11.1	0.0	7.7	0.0	0.0
Money and education	18.5	23.1	0.0	7.7	7.6
Money and occupation	3.7	0.0	7.7	15.4	5.7
Snobbery	3.7	0.0	7.7	0.0	0.0
Don't know	51.9	53.8	46.1	38.4	71.6

The most striking feature of the table is the large percentage of respondents who did not define criteria by which class could be decided. In all cases these respondents had said previously that there were no classes in their villages. Amongst those who did list criteria, money and money and education combined were the most frequently reported factors, while in general the accounts given of the factors involved in the definition of class were fairly simple. With all the villages being fairly small in size it might not have been expected that such descriptions would have dwelt markedly on sheer class differences in the sociologist's sense, and it would seem that the evidence lends weight to the view that class terms emerge less readily where people and their groups are in genuine contact than they might do in larger, more impersonal communities.

If so many people deny the existence of social classes in their villages and are unable or unwilling to define the criteria by which a person's class would be judged, it is interesting to look at responses to the open-ended question: 'To which class do you yourself belong?', which are shown in Table 11. The figures in parenthesis indicate responses to the other question 'If you were asked to place yourself in one of the following groups which one would you choose – upper class, middle class, working class, lower class?'.

Table 11

Self-Placement of Class

Class placement	Penmachno	Cwm	Croesor	Rhiw	Llansannan
Upper class	0.0	0.0	0.0	0.0	0.0
	(0.0)	(0.0)	(0.0)	(0.0)	(0.0)
Middle class	11.1	15.4	7.7	0.0	22.6
	(14.8)	(38.45)	(30.8)	(0.0)	(32.0)
Working class	33.3	15.4	30.8	38.5	17.0
	(33.3)	(38.45)	(38.4)	(61.5)	(34.0)
Lower class	0.0	0.0	0.0	0.0	0.0
	(0.0)	(7.7)	(7.7)	(0.0)	(0.0)
Don't know	55.6	69.2	61.5	61.5	60.4
	(51.9)	(15.4)	(23.1)	(38.5)	(34.0)

No respondent changed class position in response to the second question, but although more people were willing to place themselves in response to this question, over 50% in Penmachno and over 34% in Rhiw and Llansannan were still unable or unwilling to do so. The movement away from 'don't know' in response to the second question was fairly evenly shared between the middle and working-class categories in Cwm Penmachno and Llansannan, but was primarily towards the middle class in Croesor and completely towards the working class in Rhiw where no respondent claimed to be middle class.

Table 12 shows the objective class position of respondents based on the Registrar General's Classification of Occupations tabulated against their self-placement in one or other of the stated categories.

The high proportion of middle-class respondents found in Llansannan is primarily influenced by the large number of farmers and smallholders in the sample. In all the villages considerable numbers of people did not place themselves in accordance with the classes suggested by their occupations. There are a number of reasons why this could be the case. Occupational and social mobility may lead people to define themselves according to their parents' occupation rather than their own; respondents may have tried to please the interviewers, or the villages, being small, may be homogeneous across class lines. In any case the difficulty of relating self-placement with objective measures is that the meaning of terms will vary between informant and informed, but the general impression of an unwilling-

Table 12

Objective Class and Self-Placement

(Percentages)

		Objective placement in stated categories													
		Penmachno			Cwm			Croesor			Rhiw			Llansannan		
Class		Middle	Working	No answer	Middle	Working	No answer	Middle	Working	No answer	Middle	Working	No answer	Middle	Working	No answer
The same		50	35.7	0.0	80.0	57.1	0.0	42.8	66.6	0.0	0.0	55.6	0.0	41.9	60.0	0.0
Change to middle or working		25.0	0.0	0.0	0.0	14.3	100	14.3	16.7	0.0	25.0	0.0	0.0	23.2	10.0	0.0
Change to lower		8.3	0.0	0.0	20.0	0.0	0.0	14.3	0.0	0.0	0.0	0.0	0.0	0.0	0.0	0.0
Don't know		16.6	64.3	100	0.0	28.6	0.0	14.3	16.7	0.0	75.0	44.4	0.0	34.9	20.0	0.0
No class		0.0	0.0	0.0	0.0	0.0	0.0	14.3	0.0	0.0	0.0	0.0	0.0	0.0	10.0	0.0
Total		100	100	100	100	100	100	100	100	100	100	100	100	100	100	100
	N =	12	14	1	5	7	1	7	6	0	4	9	0	43	10	0
	N =	27			13			13			13			53		

Self-placement in stated categories

41

ness amongst informers in all areas to talk of social classes and social class divisions remains.

Given this unwillingness, and if the villages could be regarded as homogeneous across class lines, we wanted to see what other factors could be seen as giving rise to possible divisions in the villages and the conflicts these could engender. Respondents were asked whether they saw their villages as being made up of various social groups and Table 13 presents responses to the question:

'People tend to see the place they live in as being made up of various groups of people. What do you think about this? Would you say there were different groups in Llansannan (Croesor) (Penmachno) (Rhiw)?'

A majority of respondents in all the villages either did not know if groups existed or did not think that they did, and this absence was again primarily explained by the similar and unified nature of the population, the fact that everybody mixes, and the size of the respective villages. Typical answers included:

'The people are the same here, there are no cliques. The village is too small for that.'

Penmachno.

'There are societies here, but no social groups. I get on with everybody regardless as everybody is the same here. I don't know of any.'

Cwm.

'Everybody is the same. This is a close community.'

Rhiw

'Everybody is very similar here. More English have come to live here and they aren't quite as prepared to take part. But they seem to be enjoying themselves. There's plenty of Welsh left mind you.'

Llansannan.

Categories I to V in Table 13 suggest a degree of incompatibility and perhaps conflict, but the responses included in categories VI to XI comprised merely a listing of groups, although once again descriptions remained fairly simple and few people mentioned more than one or two groups in their villages.

The only response common to all five villages concerned the existence of a definite grouping of English incomers, be they all-year-round residents or second-home owners, and a clear and separate grouping of Welsh people. This view received its most vehement articulation in Llansannan:

'A lot of people have come here to live, English mainly, and they want to build new houses to bring more people here but we are trying to stop them. The village is the right size now and more people, especially English, would drown the place. The English are in the pubs and slowly they are taking the place over.'

Table 13

Perceptions of Social Groupings

	Penmachno	Cwm	Croesor	Rhiw	Llansannan
I English people/ Welsh people	14.8	15.4	15.4	23.1	3.8
II Important people/ Ordinary people	0.0	0.0	0.0	0.0	1.9
III Professional people/ Ordinary people	0.0	0.0	0.0	0.0	1.9
IV Broadminded people/ Traditional people	0.0	0.0	15.4	0.0	3.8
V Welsh Language Society people/ Other people	0.0	0.0	0.0	0.0	7.6
VI Chapel people and public house people	3.7	0.0	7.7	0.0	1.9
VII Young people and old people	7.4	0.0	7.7	0.0	1.9
VIII Chapel people and church people	0.0	0.0	0.0	0.0	3.8
IX Welsh nationalists and chapel people	0.0	0.0	0.0	0.0	1.9
X Welsh people who go to chapel and English people who go to the public house	0.0	0.0	0.0	0.0	3.8
XI Village activity groups	0.0	0.0	0.0	0.0	1.9
XII There are no groups	37.05	23.1	30.7	76.9	50.8
XIII Don't know	37.05	61.5	23.1	0.0	13.1
XIV There are groups but don't know what they are	0.0	0.0	0.0	0.0	1.9

A somewhat different view of Llansannan was given by one of 'the English':
'I'm an outsider really and even though I've been here for seven years
I still don't know how people regard the situation in which they live.
It's rather difficult for me since I don't speak Welsh and Welsh is the
official language of the village.'

A number of people in the other villages too felt that the dividing line between the incomers and the local population was clear-cut.

'The English mix together. The Welsh mix together. Everybody is united except the English.'

Rhiw.

'There are people who have lived here all their lives and there are those who move in here but are unable to communicate socially because they cannot speak Welsh. This is a tragedy.'

Penmachno.

The inability of the incomers to speak the Welsh language was thought by the majority of respondents who felt this way to be a fairly clear source of difference between the two groups, and in most cases the sense of difference and indeed of incompatibility between the groups was well developed, albeit in the case of the last-quoted respondent with a sense of regret. Other possible distinctions between the two groups did not, however, emerge so clearly. Only two respondents, both in Llansannan, identified the English newcomers with the "pub" and the Welsh residents with the "chapel", and it has already been noted that few respondents in any of the villages talked of the newcomers as, say, being of a different social class to the native residents.

However, the other side of the coin was put by other respondents who specifically mentioned the fact that the incomers and the local residents do mix to the exclusion of social groupings:

'It is difficult to say unless you want to draw a line between strangers and ourselves, but we are very friendly and we welcome everybody.'

Cwm.

This respondent did seem to be making the distinction in her own mind between 'strangers' and 'ourselves' but would not be drawn into saying that such comparison formed the basis of different social groupings. Similar responses were given in Penmachno and Rhiw, where the general feeling amongst those who did talk of the English and the Welsh was that although there were no groups, the incomers were somewhat different. Generally, though, the mention of groups in terms of conflict was very limited. To amplify local residents' awareness of divisions in their villages and to find out whether they considered conflict to be prevalent when asked to speak of social isolation, respondents were asked the following question:

'Are there any sorts of people who don't mix, any types who keep apart from one another?'

Again a majority of respondents in all the villages with the exception of Croesor did not identify types of people who were socially isolated in their

Table 14

Perceptions of Types of People who do not Mix

Types who don't mix	Penmachno	Cwm	Croesor	Rhiw	Llansannan
Second-home owners	3.7	15.4	0.0	0.0	0.0
English incomers	3.7	15.4	23.1	23.1	5.7
Chapel people/Pub people	0.0	0.0	7.7	0.0	1.9
Recluses	7.4	0.0	7.7	7.7	3.8
There is feigned togetherness	3.7	0.0	7.7	0.0	0.0
Welsh Language Society people	0.0	0.0	7.7	0.0	1.9
None	81.5	69.2	46.1	69.2	73.6
Don't know	0.0	0.0	0.0	0.0	13.1

villages. Of those who did speak of isolation the main mention was given to second-home owners and English incomers. Within the category 'English incomers' little distinction seemed to be made in people's minds between those who occupied properties all the year round and those, second homers, who were present only for a certain part of the year. But again only in very few cases was malice attributed to any of those who kept apart from each other.

'Yes, the English, although relations with natives are very friendly.'

Cwm.

'There are those who go to chapel and those who don't. and there are those who have moved in here to live from outside. But life seems to go on all the same. All the groups mix very well.'
'I'm not a native of the place and as such I'm really an outsider. I mix quite well – we mutually accept that I am not a native and that I don't have roots here. But the English summer home owners try very much to mix and the villagers respond very well, but there is gap between them, cultural and linguistic.'

Penmachno.

'Some English don't come to chapel, so they tend to be left out. But some do come though.'

Croesor.

'Some of the English living here, not the second-home owners, I hardly see them.'

Rhiw.

'I'm a member of the newcomer group I suppose, but everybody has

45

been very friendly. I couldn't go to any of the chapels even if I wanted to since everything is in Welsh.'

'No, the English mix very well with everybody.'

Llansannan.

For the respondents who felt that the 'English' were isolated from other people in their villages the Welsh language was seen as an important factor in this isolation, an ability to speak it being almost a prerequisite for attendance at chapel in Llansannan, and in Croesor too attendance at chapel was remarked on as important if one was not to be left out. But again these views were expressed by a minority of people. Membership of religious organizations will be looked at in a later chapter but it is interesting to note that amongst those respondents who talked of the isolation of the English, those in Llansannan and Croesor seemed to be more aware of the 'Welshness' of the chapel acting as a barrier to social interaction with monoglot English speakers. In Cwm Penmachno, English language services have been held in one of the chapels and in Rhiw, as we shall see later, the role of the chapel as a meeting place has certainly declined. Group divisions between 'chapel people' and 'pub people' *per se* did not emerge clearly in any of the villages, however.

As might have been expected, a category had to be reserved for 'recluses', people who are not identified as belonging to any particular group but who do not mix with others in the village and perhaps cannot be thought of as in conflict with others except on an individual level. This is something which is not easily related to an understanding of group divisions in the villages concerned.

The overall impression gleaned from the answers to this series of questions is that the sense of conflict in the villages is not highly developed. Local people's perceptions of divisions based either on class or social grouping are limited, and although the incomer/local and English/Welsh divide was the most frequently commented on, the view that these or other groups were struggling to exploit divisions or to score off each other was restricted to a minority of people in all the villages. It is interesting to look briefly at the way in which these findings relate to those of other studies in rural areas.

David Jenkins, in his study of Aberporth,[2] states that 'As in any community where there is a differentiation in members' incomes it would be theoretically possible to subdivide that of the Aberporth area, on the basis of sociological convention, into upper, middle and lower class. Such a classification, however, would be largely unreal, unrecognized in the speech and behaviour of local people'. He proceeds to elucidate a form of social stratification which is essentially independent of economic foundations, where 'Buchedd', corresponding broadly to the English concept 'way of life', and reflecting 'pobol y cwrdd' and 'pobol

46

y dafarn', people of the chapel and people of the tavern, provides a social classification based upon fact and upon the values of the community, a differentiation recognized in both conduct and speech. The former group, the people of the chapel denoted by Jenkins as Buchedd A, differs from the latter, Buchedd B, in its religious observance especially of the Sabbath, in respect for education and knowledge, and in its conscious practice of deferred gratification, these differences of group values and codes of behaviour being manifested in 'countless details of daily life that go without comment'. The people of Buchedd B group pay some respect to the values of Buchedd A, regarding their own conduct as a symptom of weakness, but are characterized by their easy living; it is people of Buchedd B who relax on the beach on fine Sundays and who frequent Aberporth's two public houses. It is from within these two Bucheddau that social status in Aberporth is channelled and maintained.

In a recent paper Day and Fitton[3] argue that the notion of Buchedd groups has gained so wide a currency that the absence of clear Bucheddau has been taken as *prima facie* evidence of social change, and they quote a study of Bow Street,[4] Cardiganshire, by Gareth Lewis, where the author states that 'a Welsh rural community in transition is one in which the traditional Buchedd system is being replaced by newer socio-economic values'. They further argue that it is for the defenders of Buchedd groups to prove the absence of total status in traditional Welsh rural communities and, after examining more closely the occupational characteristics of the Aberporth people in Jenkins's study, conclude that the degree of congruence between Buchedd and occupation is much greater than he suggests. There is evidence that those who enjoyed high status in Buchedd groups were usually to be found in the higher occupational categories.

In his study of commuter villages in South East England, Raymond Pahl[5] suggests that 'The middle class people come into rural areas in search of a meaningful community and by their presence help to destroy whatever community was there. That is not to say that the middle class people change or influence the working class. They simply make them aware of national class divisions, thus polarizing the local society'. He goes on to argue that part of the basis of the local village community was the sharing of the deprivations due to the isolation of country life and the sharing of the limited world of the families within the village. The middle class people try to get the 'cosiness' of village life without suffering any of the deprivations, and while maintaining a whole range of contacts with the outside world by means of the greater mobility afforded by their private transport. Bell and Newby in their paper 'The Source of Variation in Agricultural Workers' Images of Society'[6] contend that problems arise with the stereotyped expectations held by newcomers of what the village should consist of. They hold an idealized view of 'the village in the mind', and their paternalism demands a deferential response from the local people, which is frequently withheld as they lack traditional authority. The local people respond by excluding the immigrants as strangers and foreigners and interaction between the two groups is limited to symbolic occasions. There may be 'gatekeepers' whose influence may be of considerable importance in defining local people's images of the newcomers and vice-versa. Pahl sees the changeover from the hierarchical social structure which was functionally suited to the village as a community to what now appears to be a polarized two-class division as possibly the chief cause of working class resentment.

There is clearly a difference between commuters (full-time newcomers) and second-home owners (part-time newcomers), but the general line of argument must be that the newcomers with their different expectations and understanding of village life will alter the existing balance, leading to a polarized division, whether purely one of 'them' and 'us', or one based on socio-economic factors. The present research, which was mainly limited to an investigation by question-naire and was not a community study of any of our five villages at great depth, did not unearth images of divisions on the part of local people which could be seen as reflecting the existence of archetypal Buchedd groups, nor were people's perceptions of social distance based on the characteristics of the Bucheddau in Aberporth. Perceptions of social class divisions were equally limited, and res-pondents generally found difficulty in placing themselves in the classes suggested by their occupations. Polarization where it was recognized was expressed in ethnic rather than in class terms, and there are possible reasons why the perhaps expected polarization in class terms does not seem to be recognized by local people. It must be said that the more continual presence of the commuters in South East England will not be repeated in North Wales because of the limited nature of the second homer's relationship with the second home area. Again, there is not the degree of geographical segregation which is often to be found in commuter villages. In such areas this will arise because both private and local authority developers tend to build houses of the same value or rent together and these will attract people of similar social and economic standing. In the villages which we studied such segregation may arise if a purpose-built second-home development was allowed to exist, but generally the properties which have been converted to second home use do not exhibit clear-cut geographical differences from those still occupied by all-the-year-round residents.

Another possible contributory factor concerns the historical development of the villages in the present study. Perhaps, as a number of respondents suggested, perceptions of socio-economic differences between villagers in the quarrying areas have become reduced since the old schisms between the quarry owners and workers have disappeared. In the agricultural areas the old differences between tenants and landlords in areas with little tradition of hired agricultural wage-labour may have become less important in the face of the amalgamation of farm holdings.

Whatever the reason, however, perceptions of class differences in the villages studied were strictly limited. Only in a small minority of cases were the new-comers identified with the characteristics of Buchedd B although Jenkins does in fact argue that newcomers do not really meet Buchedd A people and are not easily absorbed into the group, for its members do not frequent public houses where the language is English. In her study of a North Wales village,[7] Isabel Emmett argues that Buchedd groups, presuming they did exist, have been merged as a result of the development of Welsh consciousness in response to the pressures of anglicisation and that in these circumstances the old schisms have become unimportant. To the extent that people did not talk widely of characteristics associated with either 'the people of the chapel' or 'the people of the tavern' distinguishing social groupings or social isolates, it may be the case that the old schisms have become less important; but it is not possible to be sure that this does indeed owe its occurrence to the development of a Welsh consciousness in response to anglicisation. A minority of respondents regarded English and Welsh groups as characteristic of their villages. Again the inability of respondents to talk of class or class criteria does not seem to indicate the replacement of the traditional Buchedd system by a newer system of socio-economic values. To this extent, then, our villages do not clearly reflect the transitional stage of which Lewis sees this replacement as being characteristic. It is important to state these findings at this time although we shall be returning to the question of Buchedd groups and class polarization at a later stage.

REFERENCES

(1) PAHL, R. E. (1970): *Whose City*, Longman, London.
(2) JENKINS, D.: '*Aberporth: A Study of a Coastal village in south Cardiganshire*', in DAVIES, E. and REES, A. D. (eds.) 1960. *Welsh Rural Communities*, University of Wales Press, Cardiff.
(3) DAY, G. and FITTON, M.: '*Religion and Social Status in Rural Wales*; '*Buchedd*' *and its lessons for concepts of stratification in Community Studies*'. Sociological Review, Vol. 23, No. 4, November 1975.
(4) LEWIS, G.: '*A Welsh Rural Community in Transition*', Sociologica Ruralis, Vol. 10, 1970.
(5) PAHL, R. E. (1970). op. cit.
(6) BELL, C. and NEWBY, H.: '*The Sources of Variation in Agricultural Workers' Images of Society*' in BULMER, M. (ed.) 1975, *Working Class Images of Society*, Routledge and Kegan Paul, London.
(7) EMMETT, I. (1964): *A North Wales Village*, Routledge and Kegan Paul, London.

CHAPTER 5

VOLUNTARY ORGANIZATIONS AND LEADERSHIP

The previous chapter looked at the perceptions of local residents towards their villages in terms of the social groupings they felt were present in their localities. Now we wanted to look more closely at the social organization in our study areas, to discover the range and type of voluntary organizations in which local people participate. Important considerations in this context were the extent to which village life manifests itself in and through such organizations and whether there are notable differences in this respect among the study areas. The extent to which second-home owners make use of these organizations and the restrictions, if any, which operate on their membership of them will have likely consequences for the possibilities of interaction between local people and second-home owners. Following this, the patterns of informal leadership in the five villages are examined, and the chapter concludes with an assessment of the proportion of second-home owners known to local residents.

Having already noted the alleged centrality of religion to rural Welsh life, we first looked at religious organizations to understand the differences in religious membership and the strength of such organizations in the study villages. We wanted to look at people's perceptions of the influence of religion and religious organizations in their villages and to assess the membership of such organizations by second-home owners with the implications of this for 'community life' in the areas. To begin, all-year-round residents were asked whether they attended chapel or church.

Table 15

Attendance at Chapel and Church

	Penmachno	Cwm	Croesor	Rhiw	Llansannan
	%	%	%	%	%
Chapel	63.0	69.2	69.2	30.8	67.9
Church	14.8	15.4	0.0	0.0	17.0
Neither	22.2	15.4	30.8	69.2	15.1

Clearly there is a significant difference between the numbers that attend religious organizations in Rhiw and the numbers attending in the other villages. The Presbyterian chapel in Rhiw has closed and in the words of one respondent 'some people don't go, like us, because there's no chapel. In fact only about six or seven go anyway'. The denomination with the greatest membership among respondents is the Presbyterian church, attended by all the respondents who attended chapel in Croesor, and by between 56–59% of chapel-goers in Penmachno, Cwm and Llansannan. In Rhiw the Methodist chapel was attended by all those who were members of religious organizations. The Congregational Union was next best represented in our samples, and in Llansannan the Baptist chapel was also well represented. The Church in Wales was less well represented in our samples; of its nine members in the Llansannan sample four were English-born, and of the two in Cwm one was English-born. Four Welsh-born respondents attended the Penmachno church, while no respondent in any village was a member of the Roman Catholic Church. Of the eight respondents in Llansannan who attended neither church nor chapel, four were English-born, of the four in Croesor two were English-born, and in the Penmachno and Cwm samples one English-born resident attended neither chapel nor church in each village.

Attendance at religious worship was fairly high in all the study areas amongst those who were members. Over a half attended every Sunday in Croesor and over 55% did so in Penmachno, Cwm and Llansannan, while over three-quarters attended at least once a month in Penmachno and Llansannan. The four members in Rhiw attended every Sunday. A fair number of respondents in the samples had held special positions in their chapels; four in Llansannan, two in Penmachno and Cwm, and one in Croesor and Rhiw were, or had at one time been, elders or deacons, and in all areas except Rhiw at least one Sunday School teacher was interviewed.

We wanted to examine people's images of the rôle religion and religious organizations played in their communities to see whether they viewed membership and attendance or non-membership and non-attendance as indicative of social grouping or of social distance and social stigma, and to see how they assessed the influence of religious organizations in their communities. Respondents were asked whether they attended church or chapel more or less than when they were teenagers. Only three respondents, one in Cwm Penmachno and two in Rhiw felt that their attendance had increased, while the majority of respondents except in Croesor felt that their attendance was the same. However, 38% in Penmachno and Cwm and 48% in Llansannan felt that they attended less, and this also applied to over half of the Croesor respondents and to one of the four in Rhiw who were members of a religious organization. Bearing in mind their own attendance we wanted to investigate the views of local residents concerning the types of people who attend places of worship and the types who do not. Without negotiating the complexities of the relationship between religious membership and religious commitment we were once again looking for people's perceptions of divisions within their communities, this time based on allegiance to a specific institution, the chapel or the church. Respondents were asked the open-ended question 'What sort of people do you think go to church or chapel here?'

Table 16

Who Goes to Church or Chapel?

	Penmachno %	Cwm %	Croesor %	Rhiw %	Llansannan %
No distinction between those who do/don't	51.9	23.1	23.1	46.1	16.9
Active people	—	15.4	—	—	5.7
Old/Welsh traditionalists	14.8	38.4	—	23.1	24.5
People with traditional values	3.7	—	23.1	—	5.7
Snobs	3.7	—	—	—	1.9
Good religious people	7.4	—	—	—	13.2
Farmers	—	—	7.7	7.7	1.9
Don't know	18.5	23.1	46.1	23.1	30.2

The first thing to note is the relatively large numbers of respondents, both members and non-members of religious organizations, who answered 'Don't know' to the question and could not define the type of people who attend. Secondly, a large number of people, over 50% in Penmachno, felt that there was no distinction between people who do and people who do not attend religious services in their community. These answers were typified by the following responses:

'Sometimes I think there's no difference now . . . pub people were the ones who used not to go, but now most people of the village don't go.'

Llansannan.

'There's no difference between those who don't go and those who do go, quite honestly.'

Penmachno.

'It's difficult to say, many local people don't go, even though they come from chapel-going families.'

Cwm.

'Very few attend – it would be impossible to describe any characteristics of such a small group.'

Croesor.

It has been noted that the Presbyterian chapel in Rhiw has closed. One respondent remarked 'My chapel's closed, and the others are near to closing', and another that 'very few go so you can't really distinguish a type of people who do go. Because the chapels are shutting the majority don't go.' This was a view shared by half of the respondents in Rhiw; the chapels had closed or were in danger of doing so, attendance had been reduced and this had resulted in a substantial decline in the influence of the chapel in the community. Certainly many respondents in all areas voiced regret at the fall in attendance at the churches and chapels, and the consequent decline in influence especially of the chapel within the communities:

'It's not the same as when I was young, people are not so religious; they joke about the chapel and religion, and very few people take it seriously.'

Penmachno.

'The number has declined greatly since I came. Parents don't encourage their children to come any more, and there's enough difficulties in getting the parents themselves to attend.'

Cwm.

'There's been an incredible deterioration in eight years. It's the failure of the ministers, fewer meetings – we're living in a petrol civilization.'

Llansannan.

'Everything used to revolve around the chapels but now they are closing there's nothing.'

Rhiw.

No respondent in any of the villages felt that the influence of the church or chapel had increased and Table 17 presents the reasons why respondents felt it had declined.

Table 17

The Influence of Church and Chapel

	Penmachno	Cwm	Croesor	Rhiw	Llansannan
	%	%	%	%	%
Influence the same	48.2	53.8	30.8	—	45.2
No young people go	7.4	—	15.4	—	15.1
Less people go	18.5	15.4	15.4	76.9	18.8
People losing respect	11.1	23.1	38.4	7.7	7.6
Fall in preaching standards	—	—	—	—	3.8
No modernization	—	7.7	—	—	3.8
Fewer Welsh people go	—	—	—	15.4	—
Organizations no longer associated with chapel	—	—	—	—	3.8
Don't know	14.8	—	—	—	1.9

53

Perhaps the most surprising factor of the table is that about half of respondents in Penmachno, Cwm and Llansannan felt that the influence of religious organizations in their communities had remained the same since they had lived there, and this view was shared by new and older residents alike. Two respondents only, in Rhiw, attributed the declining influence of the chapel to there being fewer Welsh people in the community, while the major reasons voiced by respondents were that fewer residents go to chapel and that people are losing respect for the chapel and what it stands for. The view of people in all areas was put in Llansannan:

'In the past people were connected with the chapel, but today people are losing respect and only the old people have any interest.'

Table 16 indicated that the main 'type' of person who was identified as attending church or chapel was the 'old Welsh traditionalist and people with traditional values'. These two categories accounted for some 50% of responses in Penmachno, rising to 57% in Llansannan, 71% in Cwm and 75% in Rhiw and Croesor of those who did distinguish between those who do and those who do not attend church or chapel. In Rhiw several respondents were aware that so few people in the village attended chapel nowadays that it was not possible to identify their characteristics, and some of those who had previously attended the Presbyterian chapel said that they would like to attend now, but they found it more and more difficult to do so and had in fact not attended religious worship since the chapel was closed. In Llansannan and Cwm some chapel and church goers were identified as 'active people', while in Llansannan and to a lesser extent in Penmachno some respondents described them as 'good, religious people'.

'Old people, the old type of Welsh, and the older residents. Very few young people go, some English, but a lot haven't learnt Welsh.'

Llansannan.

'Local people, people who have lived here all their lives and whose families have strong ties with church or chapel.'

Penmachno.

'The traditional Welsh-speaking population, but the Welsh population is declining and the English moving in.'

Cwm.

'The old Welsh traditionalists, the Welsh residents.'

Croesor.

If it is these people, the Welsh, the locals, the traditionalists, who attend church and chapel in the communities we wanted to ascertain people's views concerning those who do not attend, and respondents were further asked to identify the type of people who do not attend church or chapel.

Table 18

Who Does Not Go to Church or Chapel?

	Penmachno %	Cwm %	Croesor %	Rhiw %	Llansannan %
No particular type	22.2	23.1	30.7	69.2	15.1
The incomers/English	18.5	46.2	15.4	—	11.3
People without traditional values	—	—	7.7	—	1.9
The young people	14.8	—	—	23.1	11.3
The rootless	—	—	—	—	1.9
'Lazy bad farmers'	—	—	—	—	1.9
Those who do not go are as good as those who do	—	—	—	—	1.9
Don't know	44.5	30.7	46.2	7.7	54.7

The first feature of the table which is apparent is the larger number of respondents in Llansannan and Penmachno who answered 'Don't know' compared with the 'Don't knows' to the question of the type of people who do attend church or chapel. Perhaps respondents were unwilling to define the characteristics of those who do not attend, or perhaps they genuinely did not know the difference between them and those who do. Secondly, many respondents did not distinguish a type of person who does not attend, while of those who did the English and the incomers were singled out, except in Rhiw, along with young people in Penmachno, Rhiw and Llansannan.

> 'Those who have moved into the village, not just English people but Welsh people who would have ties with a chapel in the area from which they have come.'
>
> Penmachno.

> 'None of those who live here in the summer go anywhere. They do all sorts of things on a Sunday, paint the house and make all sorts of noises.'
>
> Cwm.

> ' "Dim ond y Cymry" (only the Welsh) go to chapel since Welsh is the language of all the chapels. Some visitors go to the church in Penmachno but that place is falling down. The church in Cwm has been closed.'
>
> Cwm.

> 'English mainly, who haven't been brought up in the same traditions.'
>
> Croesor.

'Young people, the English, and everybody in general.'

Rhiw.

'The people who've moved into the new houses, and the English.'

Llansannan.

Certainly the general impression among the respondents who did speak of the people who do not attend religious services was that this group contains a generous sprinkling of the English incomers, be they permanent residents or second-home owners. However, some interesting insights were gained concerning the relationships of the English incomers with religious organizations in their communities. In Penmachno a prominent Church-member opined that 'the Church itself is better off because it's the English who form the core of the congregation'. It is generally recognized that Welsh people, when they do attend religious services, are chapel-goers rather than Church-goers and this is reflected in our samples, and although the four members of the Church in Wales in Penmachno were all Welsh-born, if the view that the English are the core of the Church's congregation is correct then this will clearly be of some importance to the level of interaction between the Welsh and the English in the domain of religious organization.

In Cwm, discussion with second-home owners revealed that the Presbyterian chapel had (at an unspecified date) held a special English service and that out of our sample of thirteen second-home owners in Penmachno and Cwm two had attended and had come into contact, in the words of one, 'with many local Welsh people'. This points to a dual barrier operating to restrict interaction between the Welsh residents and the English, whether permanent residents or second-home owners, in the religious domain – the differing backgrounds, generally, between them in terms of church and chapel, and the barrier of the Welsh language which, when it is the 'official' language of formalized institutions such as the chapel, will tend to deter all but the most committed monoglot English chapel-goer. In fact, of the thirteen second-home owners interviewed in Penmachno and Cwm, three attended chapel and none attended church. Two of the three were members of the Church of England in their first home areas whilst one was not a member of any organization. One respondent attended as often as he could in Penmachno, one attended a few times a year and the last attended 'very occasionally'.

In Llansannan a prominent religious leader felt that few English people go to church, and that again the barrier of the Welsh language as the official language of the chapels was important in deterring monoglot English-speakers from attending, a view echoed by some of the English-born respondents residing permanently in the area. Of the four second-home owners interviewed personally in Llansannan, one attended church services irregularly and not one attended chapel. The church-goer agreed that most of the English-born people he knew, if they did attend, went to church. One respondent who had owned a second home in the area for four years felt that:

> 'No one would go to chapel just after moving in here. Amongst the
> Welsh there is a distinct non-conformist background, whether they
> go to chapel or not.'

Two residents in Croesor expressed the importance of the chapel in interaction between the incomers and the native residents:

> 'There's only the chapel that organizes in the village. It's only through
> the chapel that people meet. Since quite a few of the English don't go to
> chapel it's more difficult for them to meet.'

The other view was put by another resident:

> 'The Welsh and the English mix in most activities outside the chapel,
> but the English are slightly left out of it on Sundays.'

The chapel and the school in Croesor are very closely linked, both having been built at about the same time. An annual Christmas party is held at the school in conjunction with and financed by the chapel and although the children of all-year-round English residents do not generally attend chapel they do still go to the Christmas party. One respondent described the custom of auctioning food at the party with the proceeds going to support the chapel. This caused some amazement to the English residents who were unaware of the links between the chapel and the school. Teaching at the school is bilingual and the children of English residents will be able to learn Welsh, although this does not apply to their parents.

It has been noted that in Rhiw the role of the chapel has much decreased in the community and to this extent membership of the chapel is not a precondition to interaction between Welsh-speaking residents and English-born second-home owners with no command of the language. Few local residents attend the Methodist chapel and the general feeling of local respondents was that the influence of the chapel was bound to have declined. None of the second-home owners interviewed in Rhiw attended religious services.

A number of relevant factors emerge from this look at the importance of religious membership in the five villages. Although membership and attendance of the chapel among the older Welsh residents appears still to be fairly high, the main 'culprits' singled out for non-attendance of the chapel were the young people and the English incomers, where in many cases little distinction was made between permanent English residents and second-home owners. In Rhiw, with the closure of the Presbyterian chapel, attendance among the local population was also very low. Large numbers of respondents were either unable to define the difference between those who do and those who do not attend or felt that there was indeed little difference, certainly among the all-year-round residents. To this extent distinctions based on Buchedd groups once again do not emerge clearly to the level of being 'recognized in both conduct and speech'. In all the study areas, a significant number of all-year-round residents felt that the influence of the church and especially the chapel had declined, a view expressed by a majority of respondents in Croesor and Rhiw and by nearly a half in the other areas, and this again must be related to our inability to discern Buchedd distinctions.

The overall low attendance of the incomers, who, if they do attend, are more likely to go to church than to chapel, indicates a generally low level of interaction between the local residents who attend and second-home owners or permanent English residents in the religious domain. The Welsh language as the official language of the chapels acts as a further barrier to monoglot English-speakers in Penmachno, Croesor and Llansannan. From the postal survey of second-home owners it appears that some 3.6% in Penmachno, 10.7% in Cwm, and 11.7% in Rhiw are able to speak the Welsh language and although more owners expressed their previous links with Wales and their interest in the language, the disadvantage is widespread, especially in Llansannan where no second-home owners claimed to be able to speak Welsh. From personal interview with owners in Cwm Penmachno we found out that Welsh lessons are held in one of the chapels, but of our sample of thirteen second-home owners in Penmachno and Cwm only one had attended. When faced with Welsh as the first language of nearly all the native local residents the barrier is apparent and although most of our native local respondents could undoubtedly speak English (we did not include a question concerning this) people's wish to speak Welsh in their communities remains. As one respondent in Croesor remarked, 'When one person who cannot speak Welsh moves in, the language is immediately on the defensive'.

It would perhaps be anathema to quote figures of native residents who cannot speak Welsh, but in order to find out some indications of the state of the Welsh language in the study areas certain questions were put to local residents concerning their use of the language. In Penmachno, Llansannan, Croesor and Rhiw the non-Welsh-speakers were English-born, while in Cwm one monoglot English-speaker was from South Wales. Of the Welsh-speakers again, 61% in Penmachno, 60% in Llansannan, 36% in Cwm and just over a half in Croesor and Rhiw claimed to speak Welsh all the time, some adding 'when not talking with the English'. Over 80% of the residents who spoke Welsh in Penmachno and Llansannan felt that they used the language as much now as a few years ago, the figure falling to a still high 75% in Rhiw, 70% in Croesor and 54% in Cwm, but in Penmachno, Cwm and Llansannan the proportion who felt that they spoke the language less often was larger than that of those who spoke it more frequently.

Over 70% of local respondents in all areas said that 'all' their close friends spoke Welsh, 70% in Penmachno, Croesor and Llansannan, 77% in Cwm and 84% in Rhiw. Respondents were asked whether they attended eisteddfodau and cymanfaoedd canu in their areas and the highest percentage who attended these 'often' was found in Cwm, 38%, and Llansannan, 36%, while 30% in Penmachno and 18% in Croesor attended such events 'often'. The highest percentage of those who did not attend was found in Rhiw, 46%, followed by 27% and 26% in Croesor and Penmachno respectively, while only 9% in Llansannan (mainly English-born) and 8% in Cwm said that they never attended such events.

Clearly in all areas the Welsh language is still widely used in conversation between local people and their associates; 72% of respondents in Llansannan, 62% in Cwm and Rhiw, 52% in Penmachno and 46% in Croesor felt that 'all' the people they knew spoke Welsh as a general rule, and no respondents in any area felt that only a few or none at all of the people they knew spoke the language as a general rule. The picture of the Welsh language as the everyday language of most local residents, and as the official language of the chapels, leads us to an important aspect of the present study – membership of voluntary organizations in the study areas by English-speaking incomers and especially by second-home owners. With the decline in influence of the chapels, the generally falling attendance even among local people, the low attendance by incomers and the barrier of the Welsh language within this domain, it is likely that interaction between the incomers and the local Welsh residents will be very limited in this sphere. The question now arises as to the importance of voluntary organizations outside the chapel as channels for interaction between the two groups of people. What level of membership do such organizations exhibit among local residents and among second-home owners, and does the Welsh language act as a barrier in these organizations as well?

A number of salient points concerning the operation of voluntary organizations should be made here. Two factors which will affect the incidence of second-home owner membership of such organizations are the fact that some will only conduct their activities in the winter months and that some will only do so through the medium of the Welsh language. Of the many ways in which an individual may join such an organization, two possibilities suggest themselves. Firstly, he or she may join an organization with the intention of meeting people there and a view to establishing friendships, or, secondly, through friendships he or she may be introduced to an organization in which they may make newer friends. In both of these cases, if the Welsh language is the official language of an organization, it will act as a barrier to membership by monoglot English-speakers, for in the first case they will be deterred from joining because of the language barrier, and in the second, despite friendships with local Welsh-speakers, they will be unable to join that organization on an equal footing unless they learn to speak the language or unless the organization is prepared to use the English language. In this sense, 'When one person who cannot speak Welsh moves in, the language is immediately on the defensive'. Again, while certain organizations operate only in the winter months, especially in a farming community when greater attention must be paid to the land in summer, second-home owners, whose visits to their second homes usually comprise week-ends in winter, will be less likely to join.

Bearing these factors in mind, coupled with the possibility that second-home owners may not wish to associate with such organizations anyway (and the view of the second-home owner as a person in search of scenery and solitude lends some weight to this possibility) it would be wrong to expect too much of voluntary organizations as channels for social interaction between local residents and incomers. Perhaps they require a greater commitment to the second-home area than the second-home owner is prepared to acknowledge. Nevertheless, because selective association in voluntary organizations is one of the most formalized and public ways in which status differentiation can be maintained, and because it is certainly one way in which the interaction of local residents and second-home owners and the participation of the latter in the community can be fostered, the consequences of membership or non-membership of such organizations are important facets of their participation in their second-home areas.

Throughout this section we will be hindered by the small number of interviews obtained with second-home owners. They were asked whether they belonged to any clubs or organizations in their second-home areas and consequently with such a low response it is difficult to measure the true membership of such organizations among second-home owners. However, as will become clear, this will not prove too big an impediment both because of the dearth of such organizations in some of the villages and because of the nature of some which do exist. It is more convenient to look at each of the villages separately in this instance.

The widest range of voluntary organizations was found in Llansannan where all-year-round residents mentioned twenty-seven in all, two of which, the Rotary Club and the Golf Club, were not actually based in the village. The most popular in the sense that the greatest number of people interviewed were members were Merched Y Wawr (thirteen members, nine of whom regarded the organization as the most important that they belonged to), the Literary Society (seven and three respectively) and the Workers' Educational Association (six and two). Two other organizations with a relatively high membership in the sample were the

Community Centre Committee and Cymdeithas Moes a Chrefydd (literally 'Society of Morals and Religion') both with five members drawn from the sample. Other organizations included the Derby and Joan Club, the Women's Institute, the Urdd, various sports clubs and night classes and one political party, Plaid Cymru, with three members drawn from the sample. The Young Farmers' Club, which used to be associated with the Church is separate now. All the members of voluntary organizations in Llansannan had close friends in their organizations and in the majority of cases (83%) these had been friends before they had joined.

None of the second-home owners interviewed in Llansannan was a member of organizations in the area, and these respondents had had second homes in the area for three, four, nine and seventeen years respectively. The evidence suggests that interaction between second-home owners and local residents in voluntary organizations in Llansannan is restricted, but Llansannan has the lowest density of second homes of the study areas and also the most scattered location and to this extent we might expect a lower incidence of membership than in other areas. Again there is no evidence of second-home owners running or being members of organizations of their own, possibly to the exclusion of local residents.

The second largest number and widest range of voluntary organizations is found in Penmachno and Cwm Penmachno where respondents were members of some nineteen organizations, two of which, the Golf Club and the Rotary Club, again are not actually based in the village. Both draw their membership from a wide area, and some members of both are to be found in Llansannan. In the case of Penmachno, both people from Penmachno itself and Cwm can be considered together because many of the group activities take place in Penmachno and are attended by people from both villages. In Penmachno 30% of respondents were not members of organizations, rising to 38% in Cwm. Again the organizations with the highest membership among our respondents were Merched y Wawr (five in Penmachno and three in Cwm), followed by the Youth Club (four and two respectively), the Women's Institute (four and one), the Workers' Educational Association (one and two) and the Young Wives' Club (two and one). Other active organizations with membership among the samples included various sports clubs, darts and football, the Ladies' Guild, the Chapel Sisterhood, the Urdd and the Nursery group, and one respondent was a member of the Labour Party. All members of voluntary organizations in both Penmachno and Cwm had close friends in them and the majority (72% in Penmachno and 79% in Cwm) had been friends before joining the organization.

Only one of our sample of second-home owners in Penmachno and Cwm was a member of an organization in the area but this is not represented in the list above for the respondent occasionally attended Welsh language classes in Cwm Penmachno. Apart from this, as in Llansannan, we did not find a second-home owner who was a member of a voluntary organization. Cwm Penmachno certainly has a high density of second homes in its centralized housing stock, in sharp contrast to Llansannan, but bearing in mind the caution with which the small samples of second-home owners should be treated there again appears to be little contact between second-home owners and the voluntary organizations in their second-home areas. Neither is there evidence of organizations exclusive to second-home owners.

The situation in Croesor and Rhiw differs from that in Penmachno and Llansannan in that the range of voluntary organizations is considerably smaller and membership by local residents correspondingly lower. One resident in Rhiw remarked that 'The only things here are the Women's Institute, the Young Farmers' Club and the Village Hall Committee', and of the respondents in Rhiw one was a member of the Village Hall Committee and one an ex-member of the Women's Institute. No respondent was a member of a voluntary organization in other nearby settlements such as Aberdaron, and the level of membership of voluntary organizations in Rhiw is significantly lower than in Penmachno or Llansannan. In the Croesor sample no respondent was a member of an organization based in the village itself but some were active in the nearby village of Llanfrothen. Here two respondents belonged to Merched y Wawr and the Urdd. In Croesor too, then, the range of voluntary organizations is limited even with membership outside the village. The low numbers of interviews obtained with second-home owners again requires caution in the drawing of conclusions but neither in Croesor nor in Rhiw did we find a second-home owner who was a member of such organizations inside or outside the respective villages and the evidence suggests the membership of voluntary organizations among second-home owners to be very limited.

It has been noted that the incidence of voluntary organizations based specifically in the villages of Croesor and Rhiw is low and that in Rhiw at least the closure of one of the chapels has had an effect on the decline of community-based activities. Both Croesor and Rhiw are small villages and to this extent should not of themselves be expected to support such a wide range of activities as are to be found in Penmachno and Llansannan, but even where a wide range of organizations and activities does exist, second-home owners do not and to a large extent cannot take advantage of them. Although it would perhaps be misleading to regard a dearth of such organizations as *a priori* evidence of the decline of the 'Welshness' of a community, if they could act as channels for interaction between second-home owners and local residents the question arises as to the consequences of the low incidence of membership of them by second-home owners. If selective association in voluntary organizations is one of the most formalized and public ways in which status differentiation is channelled and maintained, one consequence of low second-home owner membership will possibly be a lack of knowledge on their behalf of the informal leadership pattern within their second-home area. Again, where second-home density is high within a village where few local voluntary organizations exist there may be an informal pattern of leadership among second-home owners, one in fact which could cut across that of local people, or which could meet it at a certain point or through a certain person who could be regarded as a broker. A number of possibilities exist in this context and in an attempt to clarify some of them it was necessary to examine the informal leadership patterns which did exist in the study areas.

It is important to state here that we were unable to undertake a full socio-metric study in any of the villages because of their size and because of the difficulty of constructing a closed group where choices between respondents could be reciprocated. Consequently the main study is limited to an examination of responses to the question:

'If you were asked to organize a carnival or fête in Penmachno/Croesor/ Rhiw/Llansannan and you could choose any four people living in the village and the surrounding area to help you, who would you choose?'

It was necessary to choose an event which *a priori* could involve both second-home owners and local residents (the implication is here of a carnival or fête as a summer event when second-home owners are more likely to be in their second-home areas), and an event which was not immediately linked with any particular organization in the villages. The organization of a carnival or fête as the criterion of response will only properly elicit information concerning the organization of such an event, but can be expected to provide information concerning the general pattern of informal leadership in the areas. Firstly, local people's choices of 'people living in the village and the surrounding area' to help them are examined in terms of those most often chosen and how respondents first come to know them, and comparisons are then made with the choices of second-home owners.

In their responses to the question of whom they would choose, local respondents in Llansannan listed 61 people in all living in the village and surrounding area. Four respondents did not list anybody, three named one person only, four chose two people only and ten listed only three. Table 19 sets out the way in which respondents first came to know the people of their choices.

Throughout, the predominant ways in which respondents had first met the people of their choices were as neighbours or through religious or other organiza-

Table 19

Informal Leadership in Llansannan – How Respondents first came to know the People of their Choice

How respondents first came to know those they chose	First choice %		Second choice %		Third choice %		Fourth choice %	
Religious organization	16.4	42.9	19.6	37.0	9.5	38.1	15.7	37.6
Other organization	26.5		17.4		28.6		21.9	
Schoolmate	—		2.2		—		—	
Childhood friend	8.2		4.3		11.9		3.1	
Neighbour	36.7		39.1		42.8		40.6	
Workmate	6.1		8.7		2.4		9.4	
Relative	4.1		2.2		—		3.1	
See in public house	2.0		2.2		2.4		3.1	
See in village	—		4.3		—		—	
Bought house from	—		—		—		3.1	
Just know	—		—		2.4		—	
	N = 49		N = 46		N = 42		N = 32	

tions, and in fact these three categories account for over 75% of respondents' choices in all positions. The other two main factors which emerge from the table are knowing those chosen as childhood friends or as workmates. The figures would tend to support the view of the importance of such factors as membership of religious and other organizations in first meeting those who were chosen. The term 'neighbour' does not imply 'living next door to' but refers in general to people living nearby and may imply a knowledge of the village and community which *a priori* would be denied to second-home owners.

A number of key people emerged from people's choices. Person A, a school-teacher, was chosen as first choice twelve times, almost a quarter of the total, seven times as second choice, five times as third and once as fourth choice, and twenty-five times in all. Knowledge of Person A was claimed through organizations over 50% of the time over all choices.

Person B, a shopowner, was chosen as first choice by five respondents, five times as second choice and fourteen times in all. Person B had been first known primarily as a childhood friend and neighbour.

Person C, an ex-teacher, was chosen eleven times in all, once as first choice, and was first known primarily as a neighbour and through voluntary organizations.

Persons D and E were wives of Persons A and B, Person D being chosen four times as first choice and nine times in all primarily as a neighbour and as a member of voluntary organizations. This was also true of Person E, who was chosen four times as first choice and eight times in all. One person was chosen seven times, two were chosen five times and five were chosen four times, but Persons A, B, C, D and E were chosen as first choice by one half of all respondents and collected between them 40% of all choices. It was clear that most Llansannan respondents felt that there were a large number of people in the village who would be willing and able to undertake the organization of a fête or carnival and responses included:

'It's difficult to say really, there are so many people who would do.'

'The same people do everything here, but remember it's good to have them.'

Second-home owners were asked the same question as local residents, but once again we were faced with difficulties because of the low number of second-home owners interviewed. Of the four owners interviewed, one chose Person A and one other person not mentioned by local residents. The other three felt that they did not know enough people in the village to answer the question and consequently did not choose anyone. One owner remarked that 'I can't really say – I have talked to some political party members, but that's all really'. No second-home owner or local person chose a second-home owner in response to the question.

Table 20

Informal Leadership in Penmachno and Cwm – How Respondents first came to know the People of their Choice

How respondents first came to know those they chose	First choice		Second choice		Third choice		Fourth choice	
	Penm	Cwm	Penm	Cwm	Penm	Cwm	Penm	Cwm
	%	%	%	%	%	%	%	%
Religious organization	15.7	33.3	29.4	28.6	14.28	20.0	—	—
Other organization	21.1	11.1	—	14.2	—	—	—	100.0
Schoolmate	5.3	—	—	—	7.14	20.0	—	—
Childhood friend	5.3	33.3	11.8	28.6	7.14	—	16.6	—
Neighbour	47.3	22.3	47.0	28.6	50.0	20.0	83.4	—
Workmate	5.3	—	—	—	—	—	—	—
Relative	—	—	—	—	7.14	—	—	—
See in pub	—	—	—	—	—	20.0	—	—
Know as teacher	—	—	11.8	—	7.14	20.0	—	—
Just meet in village	—	—	—	—	7.14	—	—	—
N =	19	9	17	7	14	5	6	2

Respondents in Cwm Penmachno listed eight people in all, seven living in Cwm and one in Penmachno itself. Four respondents did not list anybody, two listed just one person, two listed just two and three listed only three. Penmachno respondents listed 23 people in total, eight respondents listing nobody, two listing just one, three choosing two only, and eight listing three only. Table 20 sets out the way in which respondents first came to know the people of their choice:

Again, both in Penmachno and in Cwm, the predominant ways in which respondents had first met the people of their choice were as neighbours and through religious and other organizations, and to as lesser extent as childhood friends.

Five persons, Persons A, B, C, D and E were chosen by respondents from both villages, and these accounted for 59% of all choices in Penmachno and for 78% in Cwm. Person A, a retired post-mistress living in Cwm, was chosen as first choice by eight respondents, and fifteen times in all, and was known primarily to those who chose her as a childhood friend and neighbour. Person B, a teacher, was chosen thirteen times in all, nine times as first choice and had first become known to respondents as a neighbour and through religious organizations. Person C was chosen nine times in all, mainly by respondents from Penmachno although he lived nearer to Cwm, while Persons D and E, both living in Cwm, were both chosen seven times. It is interesting to note that while in Cwm 91.3% of all respondents' choices lived actually in Cwm, the rest going to Person B in Penmachno, in Penmachno itself 39% of respondents' choices went to Persons A, C, D and E living in Cwm. We were not able to look deeply into people's choices to the extent of asking why they made them – presumably because they felt that those chosen would be best able to help them organize a fête or carnival – and it would be ambitious to try to explain this difference, but it may well provide certain difficulties for second-home owners' understanding of informal leadership in the villages.

In all only thirteen interviews were obtained with second-home owners in Cwm and Penmachno, and ten people in total were selected in response to the question. Five respondents chose nobody at all mainly because 'I have no idea, I don't know many people in Penmachno'. Three second-home owners chose one person only, three chose three only, and only two chose the full complement of four. Person A was chosen twice, notably by the two respondents who had attended the special English chapel service which was held in Cwm Penmachno, and was known to respondents because of this. These two respondents chose two other local residents whom they had met at this time, only one having been selected by a local respondent. Person B was chosen once only, by a respondent who said that he had heard of his reputation. Person F, a shopkeeper in Pen-machno who was chosen twice by local respondents in Penmachno, was chosen four times and his wife three times, both by second-home owners from Cwm and Penmachno, but no other person selected was chosen more than once. Again, no second-home owner was chosen either by a local person or a second-home owner in response to the question.

Local respondents in Croesor listed a total of fifteen people in response to the question, three people listing nobody, two people listing two only and one respondent listing only three. The table shows the way in which respondents first came to know the people of their choice, and again the predominant ways were as neighbours and through organizations. Two key people emerged from the choices. Person A, the post-mistress, was chosen eight times in all, three times as first choice, three times as second, and once each as third and fourth, and had become known to those who chose her primarily as a neighbour and through the post office. Person B, a teacher, was chosen seven times in all, five times as first choice, once as second and once as third and had primarily come to be known through organizations in the village. One other person was chosen three times, but no one else was chosen more than twice, and Persons A and B accounted for 80% of first choices and for 43% of all choices in Croesor.

Table 21

Informal Leadership in Croesor – How Respondents first came to know the People of their Choice

How respondents first came to know those they chose	First choice %	Second choice %	Third choice %	Fourth choice %
Religious organization	20	20	25.0	28.6
Other organization	20	—	12.5	—
Neighbour	40	60	37.5	42.8
Workmate	—	—	12.5	—
Relative	—	—	12.5	—
See in post office	10	20	—	—
Know as teacher	10	—	—	14.3
Through friends	—	—	—	14.3
N =	10	10	8	7

Despite the clarity of this pattern, a number of respondents felt that it would be somewhat of a struggle to find people willing and able to undertake the organization of a carnival or fête. One respondent remarked that 'there's nobody left to do that although I don't know about the English people', and another, emphasizing the close links between them, felt that 'there are too few to choose – it would all have to be in the hands of the school and the chapel'. Only two second-home owners were personally interviewed in Croesor. One felt that he did not know anybody who would help organize such an event and the other chose just Person A, saying that 'I don't know whether they'd do it but I can't think of anyone else'. Again a second-home owner was not chosen by local residents or by second-home owners but again interviews with the latter were strictly limited and it would be wrong to place too much emphasis on the responses of just two people.

In Rhiw local respondents named a total of thirteen people in answer to the question of who they would choose. Five respondents did not list anybody, two listed only one person, three listed only two people and one listed only three. The only ways in which respondents had come to know the people of their choices were as neighbours and as childhood friends, except for one case where a respondent chose a person whom she had first met purely by meeting them in the village. No other account of first meeting was given and in this respect Rhiw differed from the other study areas in that neither religious or other voluntary organizations emerged as channels through which respondents had first met the people of their choice. The pattern of people's choices in Rhiw was less clear than in the other study areas. Whereas in Penmachno five persons out of a total of 23 (21.7%) accounted for 59% of all choices, five out of sixty-one in Llansannan (8.2%) accounted for 40% of all choices, three out of eight in Cwm (37.5%) accounted for 78% of all choices, and two out of fifteen in Croesor (13.3%) accounted for 43% of all choices, five out of a total of thirteen (38.5%) accounted for 58% of all choices in Rhiw. Of these five persons, Person A, a builder, was chosen three times, twice as first choice and once as second, and Persons B, C, D and E were each chosen twice. All had become known to those who chose them either as neighbours or as childhood friends.

Comments by respondents were revealing in terms of their understanding of local leadership, and a majority even among those who did select people in answer to the question shared the view that such an event as a carnival or fête would be unlikely to take place because of a lack of organization and a lack of support.

'Things like that rarely happen here, and probably because there aren't enough people here to make it worthwhile.'
'There are not many people left here now – no vicars or schoolteachers whom you would expect to organize that sort of thing, so I would leave it to the Young Farmers' Club or the Urdd.'

'It would have to be members of the Hall Committee, but there's nobody much to organize things here and not much to organize anyway.'

Five second-home owners were interviewed in Rhiw; two did not choose anybody and were both of the opinion that they did not know of anyone who would organize such an event. Two second-home owners chose just one person each, one selecting Person A whom he knew because of his occupation and the other choosing another person who was not chosen by local residents. The final second-home owner again chose a person who was not chosen by local residents and also selected a second-home owner. In this respect Rhiw differed from the other four study areas for throughout the survey this was the only instance of a second-home owner being selected in response to the question.

A number of salient points emerge from this review of informal leadership in the study areas. To the extent that a small proportion of people chosen by local respondents accounted for a large number of their choices the pattern of informal leadership became fairly clear in Penmachno, Cwm, Croesor and Llansannan, but was less so in Rhiw. Generally a pattern was discernible with which to compare the choices of second-home owners. The rôle that local organizations, be they religious or otherwise, played in local people's choices was important in that everywhere, except again for Rhiw, respondents had first met a significant proportion of the people they chose through such organizations, and if the criterion of a fête or carnival was successful in uncovering people's understanding of informal leadership the evidence lends support to the view of such organizations as channels through which status differentiation is maintained. To this extent we would have been slightly surprised if second-home owners' choices had been congruent with those of local people, except where they had met those they chose primarily as neighbours, and in Penmachno there was the added complication of nearly 40% of local respondents' choices going to people actually living in Cwm.

There was in fact low congruity between second-home owners' and local people's choices, primarily because second-home owners in greater proportions felt that they did not know enough people suitable for the task. Had we unearthed a clear pattern of second-home owner leadership independent of that of local residents, this could have been indicative of competition between them; but although only small numbers of owners were interviewed the evidence would suggest that as a group they are not sufficiently integrated for this to be the case, even in Rhiw which exhibits the highest density of ownership. It might have been expected that second-home owners may have heard of certain leading people in the community by word of mouth, but where they failed to name anybody this is probably indicative of their lack of integration with and knowledge of their second-home area both in terms of local people and of other second-home owners. Even where second-home density is high there are differences which cloud any clear pattern reflecting this high density. The pattern of informal leadership is clearer in Cwm than in Rhiw and in Cwm local residents' choices went primarily to people living in Cwm rather than to people living in Penmachno. In Rhiw alone was a second-home owner chosen in response to the question, and here only by another second-home owner and where this occurs on such a small scale it may have been due to a feeling on behalf of the respondent concerned that there were not enough and suitable local people to undertake such a task. Unfortunately with such a small response of this kind we could not investigate this possibility in any depth.

However, something of a pattern did emerge in that where there was low density second-home ownership, especially in Llansannan, a plethora of local people were chosen in response to the question although a fairly clear pattern of informal leadership emerged. Where this density was much higher, at the extreme in Rhiw, the local pattern was less clear but second-home owners still exhibited a similar response to those living in the lower density areas. Generally the evidence points to a lack of knowledge of local people's informal leadership patterns by second-home owners and a lack of evidence of competing or parallel leadership patterns. We set ourselves the task of uncovering differences between the localities in terms of the density of second homes and, this being the case, we were not conducting a community study of any particular depth in any of the villages. The limitations of the method should be stressed but perhaps once again, given the constraints which operate on second-home owner membership of organisations in terms of the Welsh language and their seasonal occupation of their properties, they do not acknowledge a commitment to their second-home area which is sufficient to facilitate a pattern of social life which gives rise to the relationships typical of the native local community.

Finally in this chapter we wanted a measure of the proportions of second-home owners known to local residents in each of the study areas. It was intended also to look at the proportions of local people known to second-home owners but the numbers of owners interviewed did not justify this. Local residents were presented with a list of names and addresses both of local residents and of second-home owners selected at random from the electoral register and our lists of second-home owners respectively, and asked whether they knew of them firstly by name alone, and then by name and address together. Table 22 presents the average percentage of local residents and second-home owners known by local respondents in the study areas.

An important point to be explained in the table is the low percentage of people

Table 22

Percentages of Local Residents and Second-Home Owners known by Local Respondents

Village	Local People				Second-Home Owners			
	By name alone	By name and address	Total percentage known	Total percentage unknown	By name alone	By name and address	Total percentage known	Total percentage unknown
Penmachno	20.7	72.0	92.7	7.3	23.8	24.7	48.5	51.5
Cwm Penmachno	5.8	92.3	98.1	1.9	25.6	64.1	89.7	10.3
Croesor	80.7	17.0	97.7	2.3	52.3	13.7	66.0	34.0
Rhiw	86.1	12.5	98.6	1.4	86.1	11.1	97.2	2.8
Llansannan	45.8	33.2	79.0	21.0	15.8	13.2	29.0	71.0

NOTE: The figures for Penmachno refer only to local people's knowledge of local people and second-home owners in Penmachno itself. The same is true for Cwm.

71

living in Cwm Penmachno known to respondents by name alone. One possible explanation is that the list of names presented referred to people in ways that were unfamiliar to respondents in that, for example, initials rather than the names by which people are commonly known were given. However, this was inevitable in that the names were selected at random and in the way they were presented in the electoral register, and this possibility does not appear to have affected results in any other area. In both Penmachno and Cwm more second-home owners than local people in percentage terms were known by name and address together. Apart from Penmachno and Cwm, Llansannan exhibited the lowest percentage of local residents known by name alone, followed by Croesor and Rhiw where the vast majority of local residents in these spatially smaller and more centralized villages were known to respondents by name alone. Over 90% of local residents were known by name and address combined in all areas except Llansannan where the figure was 79%.

The lowest average percentage of second-home owners known both by name alone and by name and address together is found in Llansannan where second homes are found in the lowest density and in the most scattered location of all the study areas. The highest average percentage known by name alone and by name and address combined is found in Rhiw which has the highest density of second homes. Between these extremes the highest average percentage of owners known by name alone is in Croesor but the highest percentage known in all was found in Cwm. Residents in Penmachno and Cwm were also asked whether they knew local people and second-home owners living in the other village, and the combined figures are shown in Table 23.

The figures show an increase in the percentages of local residents known by name alone, but the percentage of residents unknown also increases slightly. In contrast the percentages of second-home owners unknown increases substantially in Cwm Penmachno and somewhat less in Penmachno, but here it rises from a fairly high figure in any case. The two settlements are only a few miles apart and, sharing similar traditions, it is apparent that residents do have contacts with each other in voluntary organizations and their knowledge of each other is reflected in the table. The same could not really be expected for respondents' knowledge of second-home owners living in the area.

Clearly the figures show a larger average percentage of second-home owners known to local residents in those areas where the density of second homes as a percentage of the local housing stock is highest, namely Rhiw and Cwm Penmachno, and lowest in Llansannan where this density is lowest and second homes are most scattered. The correlation between the average percentage of second-home owners known to local residents by name and address combined and the

72

Table 23

Percentages of Local Residents and Second-Home Owners known by Local Residents in Penmachno and Cwm

Village	Local People				Second-Home Owners			
	By name alone	By name and address	Total percentage known	Total percentage unknown	By name alone	By name and address	Total percentage known	Total percentage unknown
Penmachno	25.9	65.3	91.2	8.8	17.6	18.5	36.1	63.9
Cwm	10.5	85.3	95.8	4.2	36.5	31.75	68.25	31.75

density of second homes as a percentage of the housing stock is in fact extremely high at 0.99 although this is not statistically significant primarily because so few areas were investigated. To this extent it has to be concluded that such a high correlation could have been found fairly frequently by chance even if there were absolutely no association in the population, although in the long run we can expect to obtain intervals which would include this correlation 95% of the time. At this point it is necessary to emphasize the distinction between a test of significance and a measure of the degree of relationship. Had we obtained a correlation of 0.99 with a sample size of nine villages rather than five this would have been significant at the 0.05 level. What is more important, however, is the similarity and difference between the villages which were studied and to this end the following hypotheses were tested between each of the study areas.

HYPOTHESIS I:

That there is no difference between the percentage of second-home owners known by name alone.

HYPOTHESIS II:

That there is no difference between the percentage of second-home owners known by name and address together.

Table 24

Tests of Hypotheses I and II

Hypothesis I

	Penmachno	Cwm	Croesor	Rhiw
Cwm	N/S	—	—	—
Croesor	10%	N/S	—	—
Rhiw	0.1%	1%	10%	—
Llansannan	N/S	N/S	5%	0.1%

Hypothesis II

	Penmachno	Cwm	Croesor	Rhiw
Cwm	1%	—	—	—
Croesor	N/S	10%	—	—
Rhiw	1%	N/S	5%	—
Llansannan	10%	0.1%	5%	0.1%

NOTES: Where a percentage figure is shown the difference is significant at this level and the hypothesis is rejected.
Where 'N/S' is shown the difference is not significant and the hypothesis is accepted.

The hypothesis (HYPOTHESIS III) that there was no significant difference between the percentage of local residents known to local residents by name and address together was also tested and the results are shown below:

Table 25
Test of Hypothesis III

	Penmachno	Cwm	Croesor	Rhiw
Cwm	N/S	—	—	—
Croesor	N/S	N/S	—	—
Rhiw	N/S	N/S	N/S	—
Llansannan	N/S	5%	10%	5%

Considering hypothesis I, a significant difference exists between the average percentage of second-home owners known by name alone to local residents in Rhiw and the average percentage known by name alone in all the other study areas. The most significant differences exist between Rhiw and Llansannan and between Rhiw and Penmachno, at the 0.1% level, and significant differences exist also between Croesor and Llansannan and Croesor and Penmachno.

Considering hypothesis II, a significant difference exists between the average percentage of second-home owners known by name and address together to local residents in Llansannan, and the average percentage known by name and address together in all the other study areas. The most significant differences exist between Llansannan and Rhiw and between Llansannan and Cwm Penmachno, at the 0.1% level, and significant differences also exist between Croesor and Rhiw and Croesor and Cwm, and Penmachno and Cwm and Penmachno and Rhiw.

Considering hypothesis III as a standard of comparison, significant differences exist only between Llansannan and Cwm, Llansannan and Croesor, and Llansannan and Rhiw.

Knowledge of second-home owners by local residents may or may not imply interaction whether on a continual basis or otherwise, and to this extent the figures provided are best regarded as proxy measures, but they do indicate real differences between the study areas, and although the percentages are somewhat complicated by the number of significant statistical differences which exist, two features are apparent. Rhiw exhibits a significant difference from all other areas in the average percentage of second-home owners known by name alone, with a considerably higher percentage known than in any other area, and it has the highest density of second homes as a percentage of its housing stock. Llansannan exhibits a significant difference from all other areas in the average percentage of second-home owners known by name and address together, with a much lower percentage known than in any other area, and it has the most scattered distribution and lowest density of second homes as a percentage of its housing stock. Llansannan also exhibits the lowest percentage of local people known by name and address to respondents and the difference is statistically significant between Llansannan and Cwm, Croesor and Rhiw. This would seem to be related to the size of the village, which is the largest of our study areas, because if we compare the statistical differences for hypotheses II and III, the lower the significance level for comparisons with Llansannan in hypothesis II, the lower it is for hypothesis III.

Despite the lack of evidence, then, of interaction between local residents and second-home owners in religious and other voluntary organizations, the villages generally are small enough for local residents to be aware of second-home owners and to know of a considerable proportion of them. In the following chapter the frequency of invitations between local residents and second-home owners into each other's households, together with the views of local residents specifically concerning second-home developments in their villages, are examined.

CHAPTER 6

LOCAL PEOPLE AND THE EFFECTS OF SECOND HOMES

The present chapter looks specifically at the views of local people concerning the second homes and their owners in their own localities. The section of the personal interview questionnaire which is discussed in this chapter, in contrast with previous sections, specifically referred to second-home developments in North Wales and was introduced to respondents with the statement:

'You may know of the developments in second-home ownership which have taken place in North Wales. Now I would like to ask you a few questions about this.'

Table 26

Would you have an Objection to a Second Home being sited in:

		Penmachno	Cwm	Croesor	Rhiw	Llansannan
England	Yes	7.4	—	46.15	15.4	20.75
	No	92.6	100.0	46.15	76.9	79.25
	D/K	—	—	7.70[1]	7.7[2]	—
South Wales	Yes	29.6	46.1	53.9	15.4	38.0
	No	70.4	53.9	38.4	76.9	62.0
	D/K	—	—	7.7[1]	7.7[2]	—
Outside county	Yes	37.0	53.9	53.9	15.4	41.5
	No	63.0	46.1	38.4	76.9	58.5
	D/K	—	—	7.7[1]	7.7[2]	—
Outside area	Yes	37.0	53.9	61.5	15.4	53.4
	No	63.0	46.1	30.8	76.9	56.6
	D/K	—	—	7.7[1]	7.7[2]	—
In village	Yes	51.9	53.9	61.5	15.4	53.3
	No	48.1	46.1	30.8	76.9	47.2
	D/K	—	—	7.7[1]	7.7[2]	—
Next door	Yes	59.3	61.5	61.5	23.1	62.3
	No	40.7	38.5	30.8	69.2	37.7
	D/K	—	—	7.7[1]	7.7[2]	—

Notes: 1. Depending on the housing shortage.
2. Depending on whether they were occupied all the year round.

Firstly local residents were asked whether they would object to anyone owning a second home in any of the following areas:

England
South Wales
Outside their county
Outside their area
In their village
Next door.

The majority of respondents in all the villages said that they would have nothing against a person owning a second home in England. The highest objection rate was found in Croesor, while no one in Cwm Penmachno felt that they would object. In all the villages except Rhiw the percentage of objectors increased when asked about South Wales, the percentage again being highest in Croesor but lowest this time in Rhiw. The term 'outside the county' was used to refer to a second home being sited in counties near to the respondents' own, and the percentage of objectors increased only slightly in Penmachno, Cwm and Llansannan, and remained unaltered in Croesor and Rhiw. The percentage of respondents with objections to second homes being sited outside their immediate area increased only in Llansannan and Croesor, again with the highest objection rate being found in Croesor and the lowest in Rhiw.

When respondents were asked whether they would have anything against a second home being sited in their village the percentage who said that they would object remained the same in Cwm, Croesor and Rhiw, while it increased in Penmachno and Llansannan, and now represented a majority of respondents in all the villages except Rhiw. Finally, respondents were asked whether they would have an objection to a second home being sited next door. In Croesor, where in any case it had been consistently high, the percentage who said they would object remained the same at 61.5%, while in Penmachno, Cwm and Llansannan, the objection rate was similarly around the 60% mark. While increasing, in Rhiw the percentage remained at the relatively low level of 23%. Significant statistical differences exist in most cases at the 5% level between Rhiw and the other villages concerning the percentage of respondents who would object to a second home being sited both in their village and next door, but perhaps the most surprising feature of the responses to this series of questions is the high percentage of respondents in all the study areas who said that they would have no objection to a second home being sited either in their village or next door. Nearly 40% of respondents in all the villages except Rhiw, where the figures reach 70% said that they would have no objection to living next door to a property which was used as a second home. The sharpest changes in people's opinions of second homes occur in

Penmachno, Cwm and Llansannan during the move from England to South Wales, while in Rhiw the only change occurs during the move from in the village to next door, but the large percentage of respondents who would not object to a second home being sited next door remains.

In view of these somewhat surprising findings and to set a background to respondents' general feelings towards second homes in their villages, we wanted to look at the frequency with which respondents had been invited into second homes and the frequency with which they had invited members of second-home families into theirs. Responses to the question of whether they had even been invited into a second home are shown in Table 27.

Table 27

Have you ever been Invited into a Second Home?

		Penmachno	Cwm	Croesor	Rhiw	Llansannan
Second	No	51.9	30.8	30.8	30.8	58.5
	Frequently	18.5	30.8	46.2	15.4	9.4
Home	Sometimes	11.1	7.7	23.0	30.8	13.2
	Rarely	11.1	15.35	—	23.0	13.2
One	Once	7.4	15.35	—	—	5.7
Second	No	74.1	69.2	53.8	53.8	86.8
	Frequently	7.4	23.1	30.8	15.4	1.9
Home	Sometimes	11.1	—	15.4	15.4	9.4
	Rarely	3.7	—	—	15.4	1.9
Two	Once	3.7	7.7	—	—	—
Second	No	88.9	76.9	84.6	69.2	98.1
	Frequently	—	—	15.4	15.4	—
Home	Sometimes	11.1	23.1	—	15.4	1.9
	Rarely	—	—	—	—	—
Three	Once	—	—	—	—	—
Second	No	92.6	92.3	92.3	69.2	98.1
	Frequently	—	—	7.7	15.4	—
Home	Sometimes	7.4	—	—	15.4	1.9
	Rarely	—	7.7	—	—	—
Four	Once	—	—	—	—	—

Penmachno : A total of 7.4% of respondents had been invited into four second homes, 3.7% had been invited into three, 14.8% had been invited into two only, and 22.2% into one only. In all 51.9% had never been invited into a second home.

79

Cwm : 7.7% of Cwm respondents had been invited into four second homes, 15.4% had been invited into three, 7.7% into two only, and 38.4% into one only. 30.8% had never been invited into a second home.

Croesor : Only 7.7% of Croesor respondents had been invited into four second homes, the same percentage had been invited into three, 30.8% had been invited into two, and 23% into one only. In all 30.8% had never been invited into a second home.

Rhiw : In Rhiw 30.8% of respondents had been invited into four second homes, 15.4% had been invited into two only and 23% had been invited into only one, while 30.8% had never been invited into a second home.

Llansannan : Only 1.9% of those interviewed in Llansannan had been invited into four second homes while not one had been invited into three. 11.3% had been invited into two, and 28.3% had been invited into one, while 58.5% had never been invited into a second home.

The invitation rate was generally higher in Cwm, Croesor and Rhiw than in Penmachno and Llansannan, except in the case of the fourth invitation where the rate in Rhiw is considerably higher than in the other areas. Generally again it would seem that the invitation rate is higher where the density of second homes is higher and this is also true of the invitation frequency. In the cases of the first and second invitations the frequency is greatest in Croesor but thereafter is greatest in Rhiw, while it is always lower in Penmachno and Llansannan. The percentages of those who have never been invited into a second home exhibit a significant statistical difference at the 10% level between Llansannan and Cwm, Llansannan and Croesor and Llansannan and Rhiw, while significant differences exist only for the percentages who have been invited into four second homes between Llansannan and Rhiw at the 1% level and between Penmachno and Rhiw at the 10% level.

Respondents were further asked whether they had ever invited a member of a second-home family into their home and the results are shown in Table 28.

Penmachno : 7.4% of respondents had invited members of four second-home families into their homes, 3.7% had invited members of three, 11.1% had invited members of two only and 14.8% had invited members of one family only. A total of 63% had never invited a member of a second-home family into their home.

Cwm : In Cwm 7.7% of respondents had invited members of four second-home families into their homes, while 15.4% had invited members of three only, 7.7% had invited members of two only and 23%

had invited members of one family only, leaving 46.1% who had never invited a member of a second-home family into their homes.

Croesor : In Croesor 7.7% of respondents had invited members of four second-home families into their homes, while 15.4% had invited members of three only, 23% had invited members of two and 7.7% had invited members of one family only. 46% had never invited a member of a second-home family into their home.

Rhiw : In Rhiw 30.8% of respondents had never invited a member of a second-home family into their home whilst the remaining 69.2% had invited members of four such families into their homes.

Llansannan : Only 1.9% of respondents had invited members of four second-home families into their homes while none claimed to have invited members of three only, 7.6% had invited members of two only

Table 28

Have you ever invited a Member of a Second-Home Family into your Home?

		Penmachno	Cwm	Croesor	Rhiw	Llansannan
	No	63.0	46.1	46.1	30.8	69.8
Second-	Frequently	14.8	30.8	30.8	23.0	13.2
Home	Sometimes	11.1	7.7	15.4	38.5	7.5
Family	Rarely	11.1	7.7	7.7	7.7	3.8
One	Once	—	7.7	—	—	5.7
	No	77.8	69.2	53.9	30.8	90.5
Second-	Frequently	7.4	23.1	23.0	23.0	5.7
Home	Sometimes	3.7	—	15.4	38.5	3.8
Family	Rarely	7.4	—	7.7	7.7	—
Two	Once	3.7	7.7	—	—	—
	No	88.9	76.9	76.9	30.8	98.1
Second-	Frequently	—	7.7	7.7	23.0	—
Home	Sometimes	7.4	7.7	15.4	38.5	1.9
Family	Rarely	3.7	7.7	—	7.7	—
Three	Once	—	—	—	—	—
	No	92.6	92.3	92.3	30.8	98.1
Second-	Frequently	—	7.7	—	23.0	—
Home	Sometimes	3.7	—	7.7	38.5	1.9
Family	Rarely	—	—	—	7.7	—
Four	Once	3.7	—	—	—	—

and 20.7% had invited members of one family only. 69.8% had never invited a member of a second-home family into their home.

Again the invitation rate was generally higher in Cwm, Croesor and Rhiw than in Penmachno or Llansannan, but it was considerably greater in Rhiw than in the other areas. The same is generally true of the invitation frequency, which was highest in Rhiw and lowest in Llansannan. The percentages who have never invited a member of a second-home family into their homes exhibit statistically significant differences between Llansannan and Rhiw at the 5% level and between Penmachno and Rhiw at the 10% level, while the differences in the percentages who have invited members of four second-home families into their homes are significant at the 1% level between Rhiw and Cwm and Rhiw and Croesor, and at the 0.1% level between Rhiw and Penmachno and Rhiw and Llansannan. Differences between Rhiw and the other localities are, then, clearly discernible, whilst Llansannan and Penmachno, areas with lower densities of second-home ownership, always exhibit invitation rates lower than those to be found in the other villages. However, the rate and frequency of invitations is generally higher in Croesor than in Cwm Penmachno although second-home density is higher in the latter than the former.

It has been noted in previous chapters that a sizeable body of research exists concerning the effects of second-home ownership on receiving areas, especially Wales. Now we wanted to ascertain local people's views of the effects of second homes on their villages, and whether they thought them to be favourable or unfavourable. Respondents were given a free hand to list as many effects as they wished although not one listed more than three in practice. It is convenient again to look at the five areas separately:

Penmachno

Just over a half of Penmachno respondents felt that the effects of second homes were generally unfavourable, 22% felt that they had no effect and 15% thought that the effects were generally favourable. Included in this last figure is the only English-born resident interviewed in Penmachno. The remaining 11% felt that second homes had both good and bad effects but that generally the good out-weighed the bad. The views of respondents in this respect did not correlate with their objective socio-economic grouping. In relation to visits, of those who felt that the effects were unfavourable, 64% had never visited a second home, compared with 29% of those who felt the effects were favourable, and 50% of those who felt that second homes had no effect. 43% of those who felt the effects were unfavourable were regular once-a-Sunday church or chapel goers, the same percentage as for those who thought the effects were favourable. This percentage rose to 50% of those who felt that second homes had no effect, but little distinction could be discerned between church and chapel goers. Table 29 shows the effects attributed to second homes in the five study areas.

22% of respondents in Penmachno felt that second homes had no effect, while 59.3% listed one effect, 15% listed two and only 3.7% listed three. The primary complaints registered against second homes were that they anglicise the community and destroy the Welsh language, bringing in new values and destroying the old. These factors have received considerable mention in Welsh local authority reports on the subject of second homes:

> 'It has brought too many English people to the village. Penmachno has always been very Welsh and if anything threatens that it should be stopped.'

> 'It has brought people from outside here with different ideas. They don't come to the chapels except in Cwm, but it's not the same having services in English.'

> 'The village has changed since I've been here. Welsh was the only language to be heard then, but now you can hear English as often as Welsh.'

Other respondents, a smaller proportion, felt that the influx of second-home owners was emptying the village of Welsh people and destroying the social life, whilst the remainder listed the favourable effects of second homes, namely that they provide revenue for the local economy, improve the housing and bring more life to the village.

> 'It has revitalized the village, more people can be seen around. Houses have people living in them instead of being empty.'
> English-born resident.

> 'It has made the place much more lively especially in summer.'

Cwm Penmachno

The percentages of respondents feeling the effects of second homes to be favourable or unfavourable were much the same in Cwm as in Penmachno itself. Just over a half of the respondents felt that the effects were unfavourable, 23% felt that second homes had no effects and just 15% felt that the effects were generally favourable. One respondent felt that the effects, favourable and unfavourable, were equally balanced. Again it was not really possible to discern class differences between respondents in the different categories. Of those who felt that the effects were unfavourable 43% had never visited a second home while all of those who felt that there were no effects were frequent visitors to at least one second home. A half of those who thought that the effects were favourable had never visited a second home. All of those who thought the effects were unfavourable were members of church or chapel, and nearly 50% attended every Sunday, while of those who felt that there was no effect two-thirds attended every week. Of those who regarded the effects of second homes as favourable, not one was a church or chapel member; one had never visited a second home but the other was a frequent visitor to two. The respondent who felt that the effects were balanced was a regular chapel goer, but only rarely was invited into a second home.

Table 29

The Effects of Second Homes

Second-home effects	Penmachno	Cwm	Croesor	Rhiw	Llansannan
Anglicise community	25.9	46.2	23.1	7.7	18.9
Destroys language	22.2	15.4	7.7	—	3.8
Hard to get houses	—	—	30.8	7.7	7.6
Welsh people leaving	11.1	—	15.4	30.8	1.9
Destroys social life	3.7	15.4	7.7	7.7	1.9
Brings too many new houses	—	—	—	—	1.9
Destroys communal values	7.4	23.1	7.7	—	11.4
'Brings bad English farmers'	—	—	—	—	3.8
Helps economy	7.4	23.1	7.7	—	5.7
More life in village	11.1	15.4	—	23.1	—
Improves housing	11.1	15.4	—	30.8	7.6

NOTE: The table indicates the percentage of respondents in a particular area who listed a particular effect. The figures do not add up to 100% because the percentages of those who felt that second homes have no effect are excluded, and respondents' choices were not mutually exclusive.

23% felt that second homes had no effects on the receiving community, while a similar percentage listed one effect. 32% listed two and 23% listed three. The primary complaint against second homes amongst respondents was once again that they anglicise the community, a view shared by 46.2% of respondents, while 23% felt that they destroy communal values, 15.4% felt that they destroyed the Welsh language and the same percentage felt that they destroy the social life of the village.

'Many young people from the cities come here and they still want the same things they get there. They carry radios around with them and

some young people even smoke on the streets. I think they are a bad
influence on children here.'

Different views were expressed by other respondents. 23% felt that second
homes help the economy and keep the native population in, while 15.4% felt
that they improved housing, and the same percentage felt that they had brought
more life to the village.

Croesor

Only one respondent in Croesor felt that second homes had favourable effects,
31% felt that there was no effect, and the remainder, nearly two-thirds, felt that
the effects were unfavourable. Of these 25% had never visited a second home,
50% had visited at least one frequently, and the remainder visited at least one
occasionally. A half of those who felt that second homes had no effect had never
visited a second home while the rest did so occasionally. Once again, those with
favourable, unfavourable or neutral views were almost equally distributed among
the socio-economic categories. Of those who thought second homes had no
effect, only one was not a member of the chapel, whilst two others attended at
least once a month, and the remainder did so only rarely. Of those who felt the
effects to be unfavourable, three out of eight did not attend chapel, four attended
at least once a month and the other attended much less frequently.

A total of 38% of Croesor respondents listed one effect which they attributed
to second homes, 31% listed two, while no respondent listed more than two.
The main complaint against second homes was that they made it difficult to get
houses, a view shared by 31% of respondents.

'It weakens the community because houses are left empty. I don't
know how but I would like to see the houses occupied all the year
round, and preferably by Welsh people who need them.'

In this context one respondent pointed out that there are no more empty
houses to be used as second homes in Croesor. 23% of respondents felt that second
homes anglicise the community.

'With the introduction of second-home owners, new ideas and beliefs
have been introduced into the village which have changed the community
and brought a new language.'

Again, 15% felt that second homes were emptying the village of Welsh
people and 7.7% felt that they were destroying social life. These views received
an eloquent exposition by one resident:

'Second homes take from the community by giving nothing to it.
The community falls back on fewer people who try to keep up the
same feeling of life in the village.'

85

Other minority views included the complaints that second homes are destroying the language and the communal values of the village. The only favourable voice was that of one respondent who felt that second homes helped the local economy, and that this kept people, who otherwise would move, in the village. One respondent who felt that as yet second homes had had no effect, was worried about possible trends in the future:

'No effects yet. We're trying to avoid it, trying to keep the community together. But there may be difficulties in time.'

Rhiw

In contrast to all the other study areas more residents in Rhiw felt that the effects of second homes were favourable rather than unfavourable. While 38% felt that second homes had generally favourable effects, the same percentage felt that they had no effects, and the remainder felt that the effects were unfavourable. All of these had visited second homes, compared with two-thirds of those who thought their effects to be favourable, and 40% of those who felt that they had no effect. Once again it was not possible to discern objective socio-economic differences between the categories. The low incidence of chapel going in Rhiw has been commented on previously, but of the four who did attend chapel, two thought that second homes had no effect, one thought them favourable, and one unfavourable.

46% of respondents listed one effect of second homes, 23% listed two and 7.7% listed three. The main complaint against them was that Welsh people were leaving the village and that Rhiw was empty in winter. This view was shared by some 30% of respondents, although one of these felt that other advantageous effects outweighed this. Other complaints were that second-home ownership made it difficult to get houses, and that the social life in the village is suffering from the anglicisation which second homes have brought in their wake. The most beneficial effects listed by respondents were that second-home owners had improved the standard of housing in the area and had brought more life to the village:

'Second homes have improved housing and livened up the village, but it is still very quiet in winter.'

One English-born resident who had lived in the village for twelve years opined:

'It has done good, broadened their outlooks on both sides. The English people want to be more friendly if they were allowed to. I don't think the Welsh people would take the cottages even if they were empty, because of lack of work.'

A number of local residents felt that the second-home owners were rather isolated from the native Welsh residents; one even felt that because the English did not mix second homes had no effect on the community, but two felt that despite this lack of interaction second homes were affecting the area detrimentally, although both said that they were indifferent to this:

'The English do not mix so the community is much smaller. I am not opposed to the English buying the houses since the Welsh don't want them. However, I am totally indifferent to the English.'

'They have anglicised the area although a small Welsh community still exists. We're indifferent to it.'

Certainly the rates of invitation between local residents and second-home owners into each other's houses does not correspond with this isolationist view of the second-home owner, but this index alone is not a measure of actual interaction between the natives and the incomers.

Throughout this section dealing with respondents' views concerning the effects of second homes in their villages a distinction has to be made between the percentage of respondents with a general attitude towards second homes and the number of times a particular effect of second homes is mentioned. This is well illustrated in Rhiw where all the respondents who felt that second homes improved the standard of housing in the area, a favourable effect, listed this as the only effect of second homes in the village, while the smaller number of respondents with an unfavourable view of second homes listed more than one unfavourable effect. Consequently, although a greater proportion of respondents in Rhiw viewed second homes favourably, Table 29 may tend to disguise this fact because it indicates a similar percentage of respondents who listed favourable and unfavourable effects.

Llansannan

Over a third of Llansannan respondents thought that the effects of second homes were generally unfavourable, while 55% felt that they had no effect and less than 10% felt that they had a good effect. Bearing in mind the high proportion of lower middle-class residents interviewed in the village, it proved unnecessary to cross-tabulate for class distinctions between these categories as the percentage of lower middle-class respondents in each category was very similar. 60% of those who felt that second homes had no effect had never visited a second home, compared with 61% of those who thought the effects to be unfavourable. Of this category again, 28% were neither church nor chapel goers compared with 13% of those who felt second homes had no effect, while 57% of this latter category and 44% of the former attended church or chapel every Sunday. Only four respondents in all felt that the effects of second homes were generally favourable, and one felt that they were balanced between good and bad. This respondent had, in common with one of those who felt the effects to be generally favourable, never visited a second home. Of the others in this category, one had visited a second home once, one was sometimes invited into two, and the other was a frequent visitor to two second homes in the area. All five were either church or chapel members, but only two attended more than once a month.

28% of respondents listed one effect of second homes, 9.5% listed two and 5.7% listed three. In common with those in Penmachno and Cwm, Llansannan residents complained primarily against the anglicisation brought about by second homes, 18.9% sharing this view, while 11.4% argued that they destroy the communal values of the village:

> 'Second homes kill the Welsh community and destroy the atmosphere of the place.'

Other complaints recorded by respondents included the claims that second homes make it more difficult for local people to get houses, 7.6%, and that they destroy the Welsh language, although the percentage of respondents in this category was lower than in all the other study areas except Rhiw. 7.6% of respondents felt that second homes improve housing and 5.7% felt that by contributing to the economy they help to keep people in the rural areas. A number of people who felt that second homes had no effect qualified their answers by saying that if present trends continue they will come to have effects on Llansannan which, as yet, are not discernible:

> 'There aren't enough in Llansannan, but they will come to have an effect.'

> 'The problems vary from place to place in the parish. Some places are worse than Llansannan itself. The majority do not attend church, although no one has condemned the Welsh language.'

Two important factors emerge from this. Firstly, significant differences exist between Llansannan and Cwm and Llansannan and Rhiw at the 10% level and between Llansannan and Penmachno at the 1% level in terms of the percentage of respondents who feel that second homes have no effect on their villages. Secondly, the effects of second homes were regarded much more favourably in Rhiw than in the other areas, and much less favourably in Croesor. Bearing this in mind, respondents were asked whether they thought second homes should be restricted, and if so, how this could be accomplished. In Rhiw, 69.2% of respondents felt that nothing should be done, compared with 47% in Llansannan and 40.5% in Penmachno. In Cwm the percentage falls to 38.6%, and is at its lowest, at 30.7%, in Croesor. Significant differences with respect to this exist only between Rhiw and Penmachno and Rhiw and Croesor both at the 10% level.

The percentages of those who do not think any action should be taken to restrict second homes may appear to be surprisingly high, but in the cases of Penmachno, Cwm, Croesor and Rhiw they correspond with those who said that they would have no objection to living next door to a second home. The Llansannan figure is some 10% higher than this but it corresponds to that of those who said that they would have no objection to there being a second home in their village. If the percentages of respondents who answered 'don't know' to the question is added to these figures then a majority of respondents in Penmachno, Rhiw and Llansannan did not suggest a possible course of action through which the development of second homes could be restricted. If these figures are supplemented with those who felt that something should be done, but did not know what, then the figures rise to 74% in Penmachno, 68% in Llansannan and 54% in Cwm and Croesor, while remaining the same in Rhiw at 69.2%.

The primary way in which respondents felt that second-home development should be restricted was by local authority purchase of houses and property, and their subsequent let, rent or sale at a favourable price to local or native people. This view was most widely held in Croesor where respondents had

Table 30

What should be done to Restrict Second-Home Development?

Action	Penmachno	Cwm	Croesor	Rhiw	Llansannan
Nothing	40.8	38.4	30.7	69.2	47.0
Council buy and let houses	7.4	7.7	23.1	15.4	9.4
Grants to local people	—	7.7	—	—	5.7
No grants to non-locals	3.7	—	—	7.7	5.7
Not sell to S/H owners	3.7	7.7	7.7	—	7.6
Central government legislation	—	7.7	7.7	—	1.9
Stronger local authority opposition	11.1	7.7	—	7.7	1.9
S/H/owners pay more	—	7.7	7.7	—	—
Yes, but don't know what	22.2	15.4	15.4	—	15.1
Don't know	11.1	—	7.7	—	5.7

previously expressed a somewhat greater concern for the problem of housing shortage in the village.

'They like the place, buy houses that are for sale – the English can afford them. The area is dying, there are no young people. The council should make it easier for the Welsh to buy houses.'

Rhiw.

'I would like it if they refused the English a chance to get the houses and bought them for the young Welsh instead.'

Llansannan.

'Second homes have caused anglicisation, a destruction of communal values and the decline of the language. A complete turn around in the values held by local authorities is needed. The preservation of the community should be the major concern of the council.'

Cwm.

This view was more typical of a number of respondents who felt that county and local council opposition to second homes should be stronger, while some respondents in Cwm, Croesor and Llansannan felt that central government legislation was needed. A number of respondents felt that local people should be given extra grants to help them with the purchase of homes, and that grants to second-home buyers should be severely restricted.

'It should by law be difficult for second-home owners to get grants and in fact it should be difficult for them to buy houses. Apart from the cultural aspect, the Lake District and similar areas are facing the same problems as Wales.'

Croesor.

'There should at least be restrictions on development grants to make certain that the places are not empty in winter.'

Rhiw.

Other possible ways in which it was felt that second-home development could be restricted included the somewhat impractical view that local people should be forbidden to sell their houses to prospective second-home buyers, and the more interesting one that if homes were to be sold as second homes then a sur-charge should be paid by the prospective second-home owner. One respondent in Cwm had a novel idea concerning the use to which such a surcharge should be put:

'They should be asked higher prices and the extra money should go to building a community centre or something. We should get as much out of these people as possible, they have plenty of money.'

Opposed to the restriction of second-home development were a number of people who further endorsed some of the favourable effects they had previously attributed to second homes. One Llansannan respondent who thought that second-home owners had improved the standard of housing in the village, felt that:

> 'Young people don't want the old houses. They want new houses in
> the village.'

One respondent in Rhiw said that he knew of numerous examples where the sellers had offered houses at lower prices to local people, but they had refused, and although he was born and bred in Rhiw, he said he had no sympathy for local people there.

With this pattern of local people's opinions in mind, in the next chapter a recognized attitude measuring technique is employed to assess significant differences in the mean attitude scores obtained from each village.

CHAPTER 7

ATTITUDES

This chapter is concerned with the assessment of local people's attitudes using a recognized attitude measuring procedure. Previous chapters have underlined a number of important differences between local people's views of second homes and their owners in the study areas, and other differences in terms of people's perceptions of divisions in their localities, in terms of the patterns of informal leadership, and in terms of the participation by local people and second-home owners in local organizations have been noted. In this part of the survey we were concerned to see whether these differences are reflected in the prevalent attitudes among local people. It had also been intended to assess the attitudes of second-home owners but in view of the low number of second-home owners interviewed it was not possible to do this. In the first instance it was necessary to decide on a method by which the measurement of attitudes could be approached and it is important to look briefly at some of the factors which influenced our choice.

Several possible methods suggested themselves. A number of types of attitude scales have been developed, consisting of from a half to two dozen or more attitude statements with which respondents are asked to agree or disagree. More important than the number of statements used is the fact that they have been scaled, selected and put together from a much larger number of statements according to statistical procedures. The small number of statements in a finished scale represent a great deal of preliminary work, and in view of the lengthy and fairly complicated procedures involved in the scaling of such a list of statements it was felt that such an exercise would be too time-consuming. For similar reasons factorial scales were regarded as too complicated.

Attitude scales rely for their effectiveness on the co-operation and frankness of respondents. Fear, misunderstanding, the desire to place oneself in a favourable light or dislike for the research worker can all play a part in distorting the results, and this has led to the development of methods of attitude measurement whose purpose is less obvious and which are intended to approach a deeper level in respondents than can attitude scales alone. For this reason we considered techniques such as sentence completion, picture interpretation, pseudofactual questions and stories, which are especially useful when we wish to penetrate behind an individual's social façade or to evoke stereotypes, self images, or norm-precepts. However, the attractiveness of projective techniques has been called into question since recent attempts to make such tests valid, reliable and scorable have met with such great difficulties that many of them have now fallen into disuse. In group situations especially, such tests are found wanting and consequently they were considered unsuitable for our purposes.

Given the constraints which operated, our wish to look at the attitudes of people affected by second-home development necessitated a fairly simple and, as far as possible, a time-saving approach. The method which was selected as most suitable for our purposes was the Semantic Differential technique of attitude measurement. [1] This technique, which consists essentially of a number of bi-polar adjectival rating scales through which in turn the respondent is asked to rate a number of objects or concepts, is examined in greater detail in the Appendix. The test was given to local respondents in conjunction with the personal interview questionnaire. A worked example, together with standard instructions, was presented on the front page of a separate booklet and respondents were asked to complete the test by themselves. The test was scored on eleven seven-point rating scales and the booklet which was given to respondents is reproduced in the Appendix.

Within the confines of the Semantic Differential technique our major concerns were:

(1) To assess the prevailing attitudes of local respondents to the following concepts:

'Second Homes'   'Welshness'
'Second-Home Owners'   'The Welsh Language'
'Englishness'   'Local People'
'Tourism'   'Chapel'
'Public House'

(2) To examine the total meaning of these concepts in terms of the three factors of evaluation, activity and potency which are seen as the primary dimensions of meaning.

(3) To test a number of hypotheses concerning the mean attitude scores of the villages, and the relationship between the attitude scores and second-home density.

In the first instance it was felt that little research had been undertaken to investigate the attitudes of native and local people towards the phenomenon of second-home ownership in their localities and that this of itself was a subject worthy of study. *A priori* it can be hypothesised that a relationship exists between the density of second-home ownership in an area and the attitudes of local people towards second homes. Again, ethnic orientation seen simply as attitudes towards such concepts as 'The Welsh Language', 'Welshness', and 'Local People' may be related to attitudes towards concepts such as 'Englishness', 'Second Homes' and 'Second-Home Owners'. 'Chapel' and 'pub' have often been regarded as bases

93

typical of divisions in rural Welsh society, Buchedd groups being partly character-ised by their relationships with and attitudes towards one or other of these institutions. Using attitude scores obtained from the Semantic Differential test it was hoped to assess whether the overall group ratings of concepts are similar or different in areas with shared experience of second-home development, at least in terms of the density and location of second homes. Tables 31–35 present the mean scores on the three dimensions of evaluation, activity and potency for each concept in each village on a rating scale of —3 to + 3, together with the respective standard deviations.

Table 31

Semantic Differential: Mean Scores and Standard Deviations – Penmachno

Concept	Mean Score			Standard Deviation		
	Evaluative	Activity	Potency	Evaluative	Activity	Potency
Local People	0.897	0.187	0.330	0.692	0.730	0.890
Public House	0.793	0.317	0.400	1.273	0.588	1.020
Englishness	0.107	0.417	0.350	0.728	0.666	0.909
The Welsh Language	1.434	0.030	0.480	0.711	0.515	1.005
Second-Home Owners	0.250	0.367	0.250	0.825	0.501	0.536
Welshness	1.274	0.160	0.290	0.770	0.743	0.877
Chapel	0.834	0.303	−0.180	0.988	0.894	1.229
Second Homes	0.260	0.603	0.290	0.901	0.535	0.700
Tourism	0.607	0.467	0.150	0.547	0.485	0.962

Table 32

Semantic Differential: Mean Scores and Standard Deviations – Cwm Penmachno

Concept	Mean Score			Standard Deviation		
	Evaluative	Activity	Potency	Evaluative	Activity	Potency
Local People	0.977	−0.103	−0.310	0.330	0.437	0.910
Public House	0.791	0.310	−0.310	1.094	0.510	0.721
Englishness	0.131	0.460	0.000	0.709	0.476	0.392
The Welsh Language	1.100	−0.370	−0.310	1.041	0.725	1.065
Second-Home Owners	0.330	0.770	−0.230	0.732	0.452	0.666
Welshness	0.681	0.103	−0.460	0.800	0.491	0.634
Chapel	0.462	−1.025	0.620	0.949	0.601	1.146
Second Homes	−0.010	0.973	0.000	0.709	0.615	0.554
Tourism	0.779	0.500	−0.070	0.642	0.546	0.457

Table 33

Semantic Differential: Mean Scores and Standard Deviations – Croesor

Concept	Mean Score			Standard Deviation		
	Evaluative	Activity	Potency	Evaluative	Activity	Potency
Local People	1.493	0.090	0.545	1.200	0.602	0.987
Public House	1.392	0.958	0.750	1.016	0.653	1.639
Englishness	0.085	0.833	0.200	1.384	0.578	1.838
The Welsh Language	1.485	−0.200	1.700	1.150	0.579	1.268
Second-Home						
Owners	−0.114	0.400	0.000	1.280	0.628	1.788
Welshness	1.314	0.033	1.400	1.117	0.671	1.280
Chapel	0.805	−1.030	−0.272	1.280	0.935	1.420
Second Homes	−0.130	0.060	0.090	1.343	0.580	1.443
Tourism	0.414	1.166	0.700	1.437	0.906	1.615

Table 34

Semantic Differential: Mean Scores and Standard Deviation – Rhiw

Concept	Mean Score			Standard Deviation		
	Evaluative	Activity	Potency	Evaluative	Activity	Potency
Local People	1.713	−0.111	0.666	0.635	0.542	1.247
Public House	0.301	0.740	1.111	1.188	0.882	1.286
Englishness	0.682	0.222	1.444	0.749	0.858	0.831
The Welsh Language	1.936	0.037	2.000	0.438	0.614	1.154
Second-Home						
Owners	1.253	0.660	1.000	0.995	0.897	1.154
Welshness	2.063	0.000	1.333	0.362	0.784	1.490
Chapel	1.253	−0.888	−1.666	0.848	0.658	1.330
Second Homes	0.873	0.555	1.333	1.061	0.885	1.330
Tourism	1.269	1.222	1.888	0.633	0.830	1.100

With the exception of 'Public House' each concept receives its highest mean rating on the evaluative dimension, which essentially measures like and dislike, in Rhiw, whilst the lowest ratings exhibit a greater variety of location. The only concepts on this dimension to receive negative mean ratings are 'Second Homes' and 'Second-Home Owners', the former in Cwm, Croesor and Llansannan, and the latter in Croesor and Llansannan. In Penmachno, Cwm and Llansannan 'The Welsh Language' receives its highest mean rating, while in Croesor, 'Local People' are scored highest, and in Rhiw the highest rated concept is 'Welshness'.

Table 35

Semantic Differential: Mean Scores and Standard Deviations – Llansannan

Concept	Mean Score			Standard Deviation		
	Evaluative	Activity	Potency	Evaluative	Activity	Potency
Local People	1.419	0.493	0.500	0.560	0.695	1.080
Public House	0.609	0.237	0.560	1.141	0.680	1.169
Englishness	0.236	0.630	0.150	0.871	0.652	1.215
The Welsh Language	1.769	0.523	1.230	0.659	1.205	0.095
Second-Home Owners	–0.051	0.597	0.240	1.153	0.738	0.936
Welshness	1.480	0.454	1.170	0.791	1.072	1.575
Chapel	1.144	0.297	0.100	1.151	1.004	1.917
Second Homes	–0.170	0.516	0.540	1.005	0.766	1.257
Tourism	0.440	0.815	0.574	1.074	0.629	1.250

Table 36 indicates the location of the highest and lowest mean scores obtained for each concept on the three dimensions.

The lowest rated concepts are 'Second Homes' in Cwm, Croesor and Llansannan, 'Englishness' in Penmachno and 'Public House' in Rhiw. In all the villages the concepts 'The Welsh Language, 'Welshness' and 'Local People' receive generally high ratings while, everywhere except Rhiw, 'Second Homes', 'Second-Home Owners' and 'Englishness' are rated lowly.

The mean ratings on the potency dimension, which essentially measures strength and weakness, are also highest in Rhiw with the exceptions of 'Welshness' and 'Chapel' and lowest in Cwm Penmachno, with the exceptions of 'Chapel'. 'Chapel' is rated negatively in Penmachno, Croesor and Rhiw, while it is the only concept rated positively in Cwm. In Cwm again 'The Welsh Language' is rated joint lowest after 'Welshness', whilst it is the highest rated concept in the other villages. 'Chapel' is the lowest rated concept in the other villages. The concepts 'Second Homes' and 'Second-Home Owners' are rated highest in Rhiw and lowest in Cwm, the two areas with the highest density of second homes. The ratings are fairly low too in Croesor, but are somewhat higher in Penmachno and Llansannan. The highest and lowest scores on the activity dimension exhibit a greater variety of location. 'Chapel' is rated negatively in Cwm, Croesor and Rhiw, 'The Welsh Language' in Cwm and Croesor, and 'Local People' in Cwm and Rhiw. The highest rated concept in Penmachno and Cwm is 'Second Homes', while in the other villages 'Tourism' is rated highest. In all the villages the concepts

Table 36

Semantic Differential: Highest and Lowest Mean Scores

Concept	Evaluative				Activity				Potency			
	Highest		Lowest		Highest		Lowest		Highest		Lowest	
Local People	Rhiw	1.713	Penm.	0.897	Llans.	0.493	Rhiw	−0.111	Rhiw	0.666	Cwm	−0.310
Public House	Croes.	1.392	Rhiw	0.301	Croes.	0.958	Llans.	0.237	Rhiw	1.111	Cwm	−0.310
Englishness	Rhiw	0.682	Croes.	0.085	Croes.	0.833	Rhiw	0.222	Rhiw	1.444	Cwm	0.000
The Welsh Language	Rhiw	1.936	Cwm	1.100	Llans.	0.523	Cwm	−0.370	Rhiw	2.000	Cwm	−0.310
Second-Home Owners	Rhiw	1.253	Croes.	−0.114	Cwm	0.770	Penm.	0.367	Rhiw	1.000	Cwm	−0.230
Welshness	Rhiw	2.063	Cwm	0.681	Llans.	0.454	Rhiw	0.000	Croes.	1.400	Cwm	−0.460
Chapel	Rhiw	1.253	Cwm	0.462	Penm.	0.303	Croes.	−0.130	Cwm	0.620	Rhiw	−1.666
Second Homes	Rhiw	0.873	Llans.	−0.170	Cwm	0.973	Croes.	0.060	Rhiw	1.333	Cwm	0.000
Tourism	Rhiw	1.269	Croes.	0.414	Rhiw	1.222	Penm.	0.467	Rhiw	1.888	Cwm	0.070

'Tourism', 'Second Homes', 'Englishness' and to a lesser extent 'Public House' are in general all rated highly. In Penmachno and Croesor 'The Welsh Language' is rated lowest, whilst in Cwm and Rhiw 'Chapel' is rated lowest, and generally 'The Welsh Language', 'Local People', 'Chapel' and 'Welshness' are all rated lowly.

At this stage it is difficult to extract a clear pattern from these mean scores. In Penmachno and Cwm the concepts 'Englishness', 'Second Homes' and 'Second-Home Owners' are rated lowly on the evaluative dimension but highly in activity. A similar pattern is found in Croesor and Llansannan, but in Rhiw the concepts are rated relatively higher on the evaluative dimension and relatively lower on the activity dimension. Tables 37–41 present the D or distance between the mean scores along the three dimensions for each concept in each village, showing the concepts which are closest together and furthest apart, in meaning. The D scores are found by taking the difference between the scores of any two concepts on each dimension, squaring this difference, summing these squares and taking the square root of the sum, and they are derived from the Generalized Distance Formula of solid geometry.[2]

In Penmachno the concepts with the closest total meaning are 'Local People' and 'Public House', in Cwm they are 'Welshness' and 'Public House', in Croesor 'Second Homes' and 'Second-Home Owners', in Rhiw 'Second Homes' and 'Englishness', and in Llansannan 'The Welsh Language' and 'Welshness'. The concepts furthest away from each other in this respect are 'Englishness' and 'The Welsh Language' in Penmachno, 'Second Homes' and 'Chapel' in Cwm, 'Chapel' and 'Tourism' in Croesor and Rhiw, and 'Second-Home Owners' and 'The Welsh Language' in Llansannan. In all five villages 'Second Homes', 'Second-Home Owners' and 'Englishness' are scored closely in meaning, as are 'Welshness' and 'The Welsh Language'. In all the villages again, the concepts 'Welshness' and 'The Welsh Language' differ quite markedly from 'Second Homes' and 'Second-Home Owners' and 'Englishness'. It should be noticed however, that D scores are not completely satisfactory measures of total meaning because by the nature of their calculation a large divergence of mean scores along one dimension will tend to exaggerate the total difference along all three dimensions. This is well illustrated in Croesor where the concepts 'Local People' and 'The Welsh Language' rate similar mean scores along the evaluative and activity dimensions, and over three-quarters of the total difference in meaning along the three dimensions (the D score) is accounted for on the potency dimension. With this in mind, however, the D scores do provide an easy summary of the total difference in the meaning of concepts along the three dimensions, although reference should be made to Tables 31–35 for the differences along the dimensions independently.

Table 37

Semantic Differential: D or Distance Scores within Villages – Penmachno

	Second Homes	Second-Home Owners	English-ness	The Welsh Language	Welsh-ness	Local People	Chapel	Public House
Second-Home Owners	0.24	—	—	—	—	—	—	—
Englishness	0.25	0.19	—	—	—	—	—	—
The Welsh Language	1.32	1.25	1.39	—	—	—	—	—
Welshness	1.10	1.04	0.52	0.28	—	—	—	—
Local People	0.76	0.68	0.83	0.57	0.37	—	—	—
Chapel	0.79	0.72	0.91	0.93	0.66	0.53	—	—
Public House	0.61	0.56	0.70	0.71	1.20	0.18	0.58	—
Tourism	0.39	0.38	0.54	1.00	0.75	0.45	0.43	0.35

Table 38

Semantic Differential: D or Distance Scores within Villages – Cwm Penmachno

	Second Homes	Second-Home Owners	English-ness	The Welsh Language	Welsh-ness	Local People	Chapel	Public House
Second-Home Owners	0.46	—	—	—	—	—	—	—
Englishness	0.53	0.43	—	—	—	—	—	—
The Welsh Language	1.82	1.44	1.36	—	—	—	—	—
Welshness	1.20	0.79	0.80	0.70	—	—	—	—
Local People	1.49	1.09	1.06	0.36	0.39	—	—	—
Chapel	2.14	1.84	1.64	1.26	1.57	1.41	—	—
Public House	1.08	0.65	0.74	0.81	0.28	0.45	1.66	—
Tourism	0.92	0.52	0.96	1.02	0.48	0.68	1.70	0.31

Table 39
Semantic Differential: D or Distance Scores within Villages – Croesor

	Second Homes	Second-Home Owners	English-ness	The Welsh Language	Welsh-ness	Local People	Chapel	Public House
Second-Home Owners	0.35	—	—	—	—	—	—	—
Englishness	0.81	0.52	—	—	—	—	—	—
The Welsh Language	2.30	2.41	2.30	—	—	—	—	—
Welshness	1.95	2.03	1.13	0.42	—	—	—	—
Local People	1.69	1.73	1.63	1.42	0.88	—	—	—
Chapel	1.48	1.72	2.05	2.25	2.05	1.34	—	—
Public House	1.89	1.77	1.42	1.50	1.90	0.90	2.31	—
Tourism	1.38	1.16	0.68	2.00	1.71	1.53	2.43	1.00

Table 40
Semantic Differential: D or Distance Scores within Villages – Rhiw

	Second Homes	Second-Home Owners	English-ness	The Welsh Language	Welsh-ness	Local People	Chapel	Public House
Second-Home Owners	0.51	—	—	—	—	—	—	—
Englishness	0.40	0.85	—	—	—	—	—	—
The Welsh Language	1.36	1.36	1.38	—	—	—	—	—
Welshness	1.31	1.10	1.92	0.68	—	—	—	—
Local People	1.26	0.96	1.33	1.36	0.76	—	—	—
Chapel	3.35	3.08	3.35	3.84	3.23	2.50	—	—
Public House	0.64	0.96	0.72	1.99	1.40	1.74	3.36	—
Tourism	0.95	1.05	1.24	1.36	1.56	1.86	4.13	1.33

Table 41

Semantic Differential: D or Distance Scores within Villages – Llansannan

	Second Homes	Second-Home Owners	English-ness	The Welsh Language	Welsh-ness	Local People	Chapel	Public House
Second-Home Owners	0.33	—	—	—	—	—	—	—
Englishness	0.58	0.30	—	—	—	—	—	—
The Welsh Language	2.05	2.07	1.87	—	—	—	—	—
Welshness	1.77	1.80	1.08	0.29	—	—	—	—
Local People	1.59	1.50	1.24	0.80	0.67	—	—	—
Chapel	1.61	1.50	1.30	1.53	1.35	0.93	—	—
Public House	0.83	0.82	0.68	1.36	1.62	0.85	0.89	—
Tourism	0.68	0.63	0.50	1.50	1.25	1.03	1.40	0.60

Table 42

Semantic Differential: D or Distance Scores for Concepts between Villages

Second Homes	Pen-machno	Cwm	Croesor	Rhiw	Second-Home Owners	Pen-machno	Cwm	Croesor	Rhiw
Cwm	0.54	—	—	—	Cwm	0.63	—	—	—
Croes.	0.70	0.92	—	—	Croes.	0.44	0.62	—	—
Rhiw	1.21	1.65	1.67	—	Rhiw	1.29	1.54	1.71	—
Llans.	0.50	0.72	0.64	1.31	Llans.	0.38	0.63	0.32	1.51

Englishness	Pen-machno	Cwm	Croesor	Rhiw	The Welsh Language	Pen-machno	Cwm	Croesor	Rhiw
Cwm	0.35	—	—	—	Cwm	0.98	—	—	—
Croes.	0.44	0.43	—	—	Croes.	1.24	2.06	—	—
Rhiw	1.25	1.56	1.51	—	Rhiw	1.60	2.50	1.24	—
Llans.	0.32	0.25	0.26	1.43	Llans.	0.95	1.93	0.90	0.93

Welshness	Pen-machno	Cwm	Croesor	Rhiw	Local People	Pen-machno	Cwm	Croesor	Rhiw
Cwm	0.96	—	—	—	Cwm	0.71	—	—	—
Croes.	1.12	1.97	—	—	Croes.	0.64	1.02	—	—
Rhiw	1.32	2.24	0.75	—	Rhiw	0.93	0.81	0.32	—
Llans.	0.95	1.85	0.51	0.75	Llans.	0.62	1.09	0.41	0.69

Chapel	Pen-machno	Cwm	Croesor	Rhiw	Public House	Pen-machno	Cwm	Croesor	Rhiw
Cwm	1.59	—	—	—	Cwm	0.71	—	—	—
Croes.	1.33	0.96	—	—	Croes.	0.94	1.38	—	—
Rhiw	1.95	2.42	1.47	—	Rhiw	0.96	1.03	1.17	—
Llans.	0.73	1.57	0.88	1.97	Llans.	0.25	0.89	1.08	0.81

Tourism	Pen-machno	Cwm	Croesor	Rhiw
Cwm	0.30	—	—	—
Croes.	0.91	1.08	—	—
Rhiw	2.01	2.12	1.47	—
Llans.	0.57	0.77	0.37	1.61

Table 43

Semantic Differential: Hypothesis One Differences between Means-Evaluative Dimension

Second Homes

	Pen-machno	Cwm	Croesor	Rhiw
Cwm	N/S	—	—	—
Croes.	N/S	N/S	—	—
Rhiw	10%	2.5%	5%	—
Llans.	5%	N/S	N/S	1%

Second-Home Owners

	Pen-machno	Cwm	Croesor	Rhiw
Cwm	N/S	—	—	—
Croes.	N/S	N/S	—	—
Rhiw	1%	2.5%	1%	—
Llans.	N/S	10%	N/S	0.5%

Englishness

	Pen-machno	Cwm	Croesor	Rhiw
Cwm	N/S	—	—	—
Croes.	N/S	N/S	—	—
Rhiw	5%	10%	N/S	—
Llans.	N/S	N/S	N/S	10%

The Welsh Language

	Pen-machno	Cwm	Croesor	Rhiw
Cwm	N/S	—	—	—
Croes.	N/S	N/S	—	—
Rhiw	5%	2.5%	N/S	—
Llans.	5%	0.5%	N/S	N/S

Welshness

	Pen-machno	Cwm	Croesor	Rhiw
Cwm	2.5%	—	—	—
Croes.	N/S	10%	—	—
Rhiw	0.5%	0.05%	5%	—
Llans.	N/S	0.5%	N/S	0.5%

Local People

	Pen-machno	Cwm	Croesor	Rhiw
Cwm	N/S	—	—	—
Croes.	10%	0.5%	—	—
Rhiw	0.5%	0.5%	N/S	—
Llans.	0.5%	0.5%	N/S	N/S

Chapel

	Pen-machno	Cwm	Croesor	Rhiw
Cwm	N/S	—	—	—
Croes.	N/S	N/S	—	—
Rhiw	N/S	5%	N/S	—
Llans.	N/S	2.5%	N/S	N/S

Public House

	Pen-machno	Cwm	Croesor	Rhiw
Cwm	N/S	—	—	—
Croes.	10%	10%	—	—
Rhiw	N/S	N/S	2.5%	—
Llans.	N/S	N/S	2.5%	N/S

Tourism

	Pen-machno	Cwm	Croesor	Rhiw
Cwm	N/S	—	—	—
Croes.	N/S	N/S	—	—
Rhiw	1%	5%	10%	—
Llans.	N/S	10%	N/S	0.5%

NOTE: Where a percentage figure is shown the difference is significant at this level. Where 'N/S' is shown the difference is not significant.

Table 42 presents the D scores between the villages for each concept along the three dimensions. The concepts 'The Welsh Language', 'Welshness', and 'Second-Home Owners' exhibit their closest total meaning in Croesor and Llansannan, whilst 'Public House', 'Chapel' and 'Second Homes' are closest in meaning in Llansannan and Penmachno. 'Englishness' is closest in total meaning in Llansannan and Cwm, 'Local People' in Croesor and Rhiw and 'Tourism' in Penmachno and Cwm. The concepts 'Second-Home Owners', 'Englishness', 'Tourism', 'Welshness', 'The Welsh Language' and 'Chapel' are furthest away in meaning in Cwm Penmachno and Rhiw, whilst 'Local People' is furthest in meaning in Cwm and Llansannan, 'Public House' in Cwm and Croesor, and 'Second Homes' in Croesor and Rhiw. It is interesting to note here that no concepts exhibit their closest meaning in Rhiw and Cwm, areas with a similar high density of second homes, nor in Penmachno and Croesor, areas with a similar medium density.

The D or distance scores do not employ the standard deviations shown in Tables 31–35, but the standard deviation is of great importance in the testing of hypotheses concerning the differences between the mean scores obtained for the concepts. We wanted to find out whether attitudes towards the selected concepts measured on the evaluative dimension were significantly different between villages, and to this end the following hypotheses concerning the scores obtained in the villages were tested.

Hypothesis One

That there is no difference between the mean scores obtained on the evaluative dimension between each pair of villages for each concept.

Hypothesis Two

That there is no difference between the mean scores obtained on the activity and potency dimensions between each pair of villages for the concepts 'Second Homes' and 'Second-Home Owners'.

The relevant data for Hypothesis One are summarized in Table 43. It is convenient to discuss these results under the headings of the concepts tested.

Local People

The differences between the mean scores on the evaluative dimension are not significant between Croesor, Llansannan or Rhiw, nor between Penmachno and Cwm. The mean scores are significantly higher, and 'Local People' are evaluated more highly in Croesor, Rhiw and Llansannan than in Penmachno and Cwm Penmachno.

Table 44

Semantic Differential: Correlations of Density of Second Homes with Evaluative Means

| | Correlation Coefficient | |
	r	r^2
Second Homes	0.549	0.301
Second-Home Owners	0.687	0.472
Tourism	0.754	0.569
Englishness	0.424	0.180
The Welsh Language	−0.208	0.043
Welshness	−0.028	0.001
Local People	0.121	0.015
Chapel	−0.281	0.079
Public House	−0.172	0.030

The Welsh Language

This is evaluated significantly more highly in Rhiw and Llansannan than in Penmachno and Cwm.

Welshness

This is evaluated significantly more highly in all the villages than in Cwm, and more highly in Rhiw than in Penmachno and Llansannan.

Chapel

This is evaluated significantly more highly in both Rhiw and Llansannan than in Cwm.

Second-Home Owners

'Second-Home Owners' are evaluated significantly more highly in Rhiw than in any of the other villages with a lower density of second-home ownership, and significantly more highly in Cwm Penmachno than Llansannan, with respective ownership rates of 51.8% and 8.9%.

Second Homes

These are evaluated significantly more highly in Rhiw than in all the other villages, and significantly more highly in Penmachno than Llansannan.

Englishness

'Englishness' is evaluated significantly more highly in Rhiw than in Penmachno, Cwm and Llansannan.

Tourism

This is evaluated significantly more highly in Rhiw than in all the other villages and significantly more highly in Cwm Penmachno than in Llansannan.

Public House

This is evaluated significantly more highly in Croesor than in any of the other villages.

The pattern which emerges from the testing of Hypothesis One is quite complicated and no consistently clear pattern is to be found concerning the evaluation of the concepts by local people in the five localities. The evaluative dimension essentially measures like and dislike, and it may be expected that where second homes are found in greater density the attitudes of local people to such concepts as 'Second Homes' and 'Second-Home Owners' will differ from those to be found where second homes are in lesser density. The mean scores on the evaluative dimension for each concept were correlated with the density of second homes as a percentage of the housing stocks in the five villages and the correlations are shown in Table 44. The concepts 'Second-Home Owners', 'Second Homes', 'Tourism', 'Englishness' and 'Local People' are all positively correlated while 'Chapel', 'The Welsh Language', 'Public House' and 'Welshness' are negatively correlated. The square of the correlation coefficient (r^2) can be interpreted as the proportion of the total variation in the mean evaluative score that is explained by the density of second-home ownership in the village. By 'explained', of course, we do not imply a causal explanation, but merely an association between the two variables. The highest positive correlation of density is with 'Tourism' and only in this case does the r^2 exceed 50%. The highest negative correlation is with 'Chapel', but here the r^2 does not exceed 10%. Nevertheless it is perhaps significant that while the coefficients for 'Second Homes' and 'Second-Home Owners' are positive, those for 'Welshness', 'The Welsh Language' and 'Chapel' are negative, possibly indicative of the greater acceptance and accommodation of second homes in those areas of greater density. However, bearing in mind that only five villages were studied, that Rhiw exhibits the highest mean scores on the evaluative dimension for all the concepts with the exception of 'Public House', and the inconsistency of the mean ratings between the areas of high ownership density, Cwm and Rhiw, the results remain ambiguous. This impression of ambiguity is reinforced when we look at the results of correlations between the mean scores on the evaluative dimension of 'Second Homes', 'Second-Home Owners' and 'Englishness' with an index of ethnic orientation, a proxy measure of which is obtained from the average of the mean scores on the evaluative dimension for 'Welshness' and 'The Welsh Language'. These are shown in Table 45, and all three are unexpectedly highly and positively correlated with this index of ethnic orientation. It is obviously difficult to explain such findings, and they underline the problem faced when scores from only five localities are correlated. The correlation coefficient is highly affected by an extreme score in either ethnic orientation or 'Second Homes', 'Second-Home Owners' and 'Englishness'.

Table 45
Semantic Differential: Correlations of Ethnic Orientation with Selected Concepts

	Second Homes	Second-Home Owners	Englishness
r	0.643	0.511	0.574
r^2	0.414	0.261	0.330

The relevant data for Hypothesis Two are shown in Table 46.

Table 46
Hypothesis Two: Differences between Means-Potency and Activity Dimensions

Potency

	Second Homes					Second-Home Owners			
	Pen-machno	Cwm	Croesor	Rhiw		Pen-machno	Cwm	Croesor	Rhiw
Cwm	N/S	—	—	—	Cwm	2.5%	—	—	—
Croes.	N/S	N/S	—	—	Croes.	N/S	N/S	—	—
Rhiw	5%	1%	5%	—	Rhiw	5%	1%	10%	—
Llans.	N/S	2.5%	N/S	10%	Llans.	N/S	5%	N/S	5%

Activity

	Second Homes					Second-Home Owners			
	Pen-machno	Cwm	Croesor	Rhiw		Pen-machno	Cwm	Croesor	Rhiw
Cwm	10%	—	—	—	Cwm	1%	—	—	—
Croes.	2.5%	0.5%	—	—	Croes.	N/S	10%	—	—
Rhiw	N/S	N/S	10%	—	Rhiw	N/S	N/S	N/S	—
Llans.	N/S	2.5%	5%	N/S	Llans.	10%	N/S	N/S	N/S

NOTE: Where a percentage figure is shown the difference is significant at this level. Where 'N/S' is shown the difference is not significant.

The mean scores on the potency dimension for 'Second Homes' are significantly higher in Rhiw than in all the other villages and significantly higher in Llansannan than in Cwm Penmachno. The mean scores on the activity dimension are significantly higher in all the study areas than in Croesor, and significantly higher in Cwm than in Penmachno and Llansannan. The mean scores on the potency dimension for 'Second-Home Owners' are significantly higher in Rhiw than in all the other areas, and in Llansannan and Penmachno than in Cwm. On the activity dimension the mean scores are significantly higher in Cwm Penmachno than in Penmachno, Croesor and Llansannan.

A number of points emerge here. Whereas 'Second Homes' and 'Second-Home Owners' are rated as very potent in Rhiw, they are rated least potent in Cwm Penmachno. In fact they are regarded as significantly more potent in Llansannan, with a density of ownership only one-sixth that of Cwm. On the activity dimension, however, they are rated significantly higher in Cwm than in Penmachno, Croesor and Llansannan, but no significant difference exists between the mean scores in Cwm and Rhiw. It is difficult again to extract a pattern and this is underlined by the correlations shown in Table 47 which are again quite low, with the exception of that of 'Second-Home Owners' on the activity dimension with the density of ownership in the villages.

Table 47

Semantic Differential: Correlation of Density of Second Homes with Activity and Potency Means for Second Homes and Second-Home Owners

| | Second Homes | | Second-Home Owners | |
	r	r^2	r	r^2
Potency	0.203	0.041	0.170	0.029
Activity	0.337	0.114	0.527	0.278

At the beginning of this chapter the main concerns of the attitude survey were outlined. As might have been expected one pattern does emerge. The mean scores on the evaluative dimension, which essentially measures like and dislike, are universally higher for the concepts 'The Welsh Language', 'Welshness', 'Chapel' and 'Local People' than for 'Second Homes', 'Second-Home Owners' and 'Englishness'. The D scores show that such concepts as 'The Welsh Language' and 'Welshness' are close in total meaning, as are 'Second Homes', 'Second-Home Owners' and 'Englishness', but these two sets of concepts differ quite markedly from each other in this respect. However, it must be said that no clear and consistent pattern in the relationship between attitudes on the evaluative dimension and the density of second-home ownership is discernible. The mean scores in attitudes of local people towards second homes and their owners as measured by the semantic differential. Indeed the mean scores in Llansannan, Croesor and Cwm exhibit greater similarities for 'Second Homes' and 'Second-Home Owners' than do the means in Rhiw and Cwm. Again the mean scores obtained in the villages with a smaller density do not exhibit sufficient similarities to justify support for the view that density exercises a causal effect on the attitudes of local people. The mean scores and their correlation with density do not indicate a 'cut-off point' in terms of density above which the prevailing attitude of local people changes from one of indifference or acceptance to one of antagonism. Indeed the positive correlations of 'Second Homes', 'Second-Home Owners' and 'Englishness' with density and the negative correlations of 'The Welsh Language' and 'Welshness' may be interpreted as indicating that as the density of second-home ownership increases so does the degree of acceptance and accommodation of second homes and their owners by local people. This, however, would seem to conflict with the positive correlations of attitudes towards 'Second Homes', 'Second-Home Owners' and 'Englishness' with the index of ethnic orientation. While what may be called the scatter of second homes in the localities is not so easily quantifiable as their density, the prevailing attitudes in Llansannan, where second homes are fairly widely scattered, are somewhat less favourable both towards 'Second Homes' and 'Second-Home Owners' than in Cwm Penmachno, where second homes are much more centrally located. Nevertheless, so few statistically significant differences exist between the mean scores for 'Second Homes' and 'Second-Home Owners' that the relationship between the location and scatter of second homes and the attitudes of local people remains rather unclear.

On the activity dimension, second homes and their owners are rated fairly highly in all the villages, and the relationship of density to this is again unclear, for the scores in Llansannan and Rhiw are very similar. On the potency dimension, second homes and their owners are rated highly in Rhiw, but much more lowly in Cwm, and the correlation coefficients show the relationship of the means on the potency dimension with density to be quite low.

In short, the attitudes of local people, as measured by the semantic differential, do not exhibit a consistent relationship with the density of second homes as a percentage of the housing stock, and it would seem that we will have to look more widely to find factors which, perhaps in combination with this density, can better lead to an understanding of the prevalent attitudes of local people to the phenomenon of second-home ownership in their villages.

Rhiw and Cwm do not exhibit sufficient similarities to allow any conclusions to be drawn concerning a uniform effect of high density ownership on the

REFERENCES

(1) Osgood, C. E., Suci, G. J., and Tannenbaum, P. H. (1957). *The Measurement of Meaning*, *Urbana, Illinois*, University of Illinois Press.

(2) The Generalized Distance Formula of solid geometry states that:

$$Dil = \sqrt{\sum_{j} dil^2}$$

where:

Dil is the linear distance between the points on the semantic space representing concepts i and l.

dil is the algebraic difference between the co-ordinates of i and l on the same dimension, j. The summation is over k dimensions.

CHAPTER 8

SECOND HOMES IN PERSPECTIVE

It was noted previously that the present study was not a community study *per se* of any of the villages involved. Because we chose to look at five localities the field with which we were able to concern ourselves was unavoidably a narrow one, and no claim could be made that the methods of investigation used could remove the need for more detailed research into areas of North Wales. This area presents the researcher with an opportunity to examine the impact of change and the adjustments of the local community within a region which is still markedly rural and non-industrial, with a distinctive and regional character, and it is to be hoped that it will continue to stimulate such interest. However, we do not claim to have studied any village in sufficient depth to provide a convincing account of all or even many of the facets of its social life. The present study was of necessity an exploratory one and we have been unable to contribute greatly to many of the major areas of interest which have been the concern of more detailed investigations of a community study nature. Five areas were chosen primarily in the hope that it would be possible to apply our findings more generally to other areas in North Wales than would have been the case even if we had been able to study one or more areas in greater depth, based predominantly on the index of the density of second homes as a percentage of the local housing stock. With the forementioned constraints in mind we have tried to isolate some of the factors involved in assessing the impact of second-home developments on receiving areas, and to ascertain the reactions and attitudes of local people to the influx of people, different both culturally and linguistically, into their localities for periods of little more than three months of the year. The following discussion attempts to pull together the themes of the previous chapters and to indicate possible fruitful avenues for further research.

It is valuable to attempt to describe the process by which the traditional way of life in Welsh rural areas can be broken down and disintegrate following economic decline and the part-time occupation of properties by second-home owners. Perhaps the commonly held view would incorporate such features as:

(1) The original out-movement of population from an area in response to a lack of employment opportunities following the decline of such traditional industries as slate quarrying, or the amalgamation of farm holdings.

(2) The in-movement of another population, employed elsewhere, who purchase or rent a second property in the area mainly for leisure

purposes. This population is predominantly English-speaking in contrast to the remaining previous population who are mainly Welsh-speaking.

(3) Depending on the character of the area in question certain types of properties will be occupied by the new population – in agricultural areas perhaps older farmhouses corresponding to the stereotyped view of a second home as a property in a countryfied and rather rustic setting, but in quarrying areas perhaps mainly terraced cottages which previously housed those who worked in the industry.

(4) With the original outflow of population those that remain will generally be the elderly, because it will have been the younger, more economically active people who left in the greater proportions to seek a better standard of living. In the quarrying areas this elderly population will be living side by side with the newer population when they are in residence, and living next door to empty houses when they are not. In the agricultural areas the properties used as second homes may be more akin to the popular view, more isolated and perhaps with a certain amount of accompanying land. In either or both of these cases younger people who wish to purchase properties may be frustrated in their attempts because of the greater purchasing power of potential second-homers in the local housing market.

(5) The traditional institutions of the area and its services will be faced with a changing situation based partly on the fact of the original outflow of population and partly on the nature of the second-homer's occupancy of property. Perhaps for three-quarters of the year services will be providing for a much reduced population and they may have to reduce their operating level. The chapel and other village organizations will be catering for a reduced membership and the frequency of services and meetings may be reduced. Even when they are in residence the newer population may not become involved in these activities because of linguistic and cultural barriers. In the final analysis the area's services and institutions may be forced to close down altogether.

(6) The remaining original population may react with hostility to the newer population with its different life-style, perhaps falsely blaming the symptom of the decline (the occupancy of properties as second homes) rather than the cause (the decline of the basic industries which first gave life to the area). This hostility may increase where examples of the inability of younger people to compete in

the local housing market are identified, and where the decline in the level of services in the area accelerates as a consequence. An increasingly dissatisfying and frustrating situation for the remaining original population may thus be perpetuated, which probably contains within itself the seeds of the wish to leave for both economic and social reasons, and as the proportion of second homes in the housing stock increases and the all-year-round population decreases, the further decline of institutions and services serving a declining number of people will further reinforce the chain of events. (If we pursue the organic analogy we now see second homes more as a complication of the original disease of economic decline rather than merely a symptom of it.)

This description is certainly not an exhaustive one but it does contain many of the features of what is perhaps the accepted view of the sequence of events which may be expected and it provides the basis for hypotheses concerning the response of the remaining original population to the phenomenon of second-home ownership in their areas. Two such hypotheses concerning the density of second-home ownership suggest themselves:

(1) Where there is a low density of second-home ownership the original native population will be unaware of the potential threat that it poses to the 'traditional way of life', and in these areas the prevailing attitudes of local people will generally be more favourable (less hostile) towards second homes and their owners than in areas where they are to be found in greater density.

(2) In areas of low density ownership (where economic decline has not occurred to such an extent) people will still identify with the 'traditional way of life' with its integral organizations and institutions and react against what they regard as a potential threat to it from second homes. Consequently their attitudes towards second homes are less favourable (more hostile) than those typical of people in high density areas where the prevailing attitude amongst the remaining elderly original population (those perhaps least able and most entitled to object) is one of accommodation and acceptance.

Taking these hypotheses as a starting point, we saw in Chapter 6 and in Chapter 7, which was concerned with the measurement of attitudes using the semantic differential test, that the effect of density on the prevalent attitudes of local people towards second homes and their owners is not a uniform one. The findings of Chapter 7 did not exclusively confirm or reject either of these hypotheses and we concluded that we should have to look for significant differences amongst our villages other than density of second-home ownership alone.

Two of the most significant differences which did arise amongst the five localities were those concerning the range and type of local voluntary organizations to be found in the respective areas and differences concerning the nature of informal leadership patterns as understood by respondents' choices of people to organize a carnival or fête in their villages. We noticed how frequently people had come to know those that they chose through membership of religious and other voluntary associations, and if we regard selective association in voluntary organizations as one of the primary ways in which status differentiation can be channelled and maintained then in the absence of such organizations the patterns of leadership in an area may tend to become more diffuse. Where a fairly clear pattern of informal leadership exists it will be reinforced in and through these associations and organizations, the vibrancy of which may in itself be an indication of the strength and resilience of the particularly Welsh nature of an area, and they will provide the medium through which the traditional lifestyle is reinforced and maintained. In this way opposition and resistance to social change in general and to second-home ownership in particular can be generated and articulated. Where the traditional lifestyle is not overtly expressed in such a way and its associated organizations and institutions are less than active, a structure for the generation and expression of opposition is unavailable, leading perhaps to a passive if grudging accommodation, acceptance and adaptation.

The number and variety of voluntary organizations found in Rhiw is less than in the other villages. One chapel has closed, and if we regard the school in Penmachno as serving the people of Cwm, Rhiw was the only village without the services of a village school. The pattern of informal leadership is more diffuse than those of the other villages, and the prevalent attitude towards second homes and their owners is most favourable here. The 'indifference' with which a number of respondents in Rhiw professed to regard the incomers is perhaps a passive reaction for it does not necessarily imply a greater degree of interaction. However, since other than on the personal level opposition has little readily available structure through which it can be articulated, nor can the older lifestyle be adhered to within the chapel and other associated voluntary organizations, the tendency may well be towards accommodation and acceptance.

Although the density of second homes in Cwm Penmachno and Rhiw is quite similar, the pattern of local people's attitudes varies quite markedly, and so the question arises as to the relationship between the density of second homes in a locality and the number and range of local voluntary organizations that will remain. Is there a relationship between this density and the inability of the old institutions to resist? Apart from other agents of social change which should be considered, and without attributing an initial causal effect to second homes, common sense would suggest that this is generally likely to be the case, although not to the extent of there being a direct and precise relationship. Rather than arguing that social collapse has taken place to a greater degree in Rhiw than in Cwm, it may be more true to suggest that were it not for the proximity of Penmachno itself, which has shared a common historical tradition, the decline in Cwm would be even more advanced. Penmachno provides a number of the amenities which can keep people in Cwm, including chapel and church, the school and two public houses. Rhiw, on the other hand, is more isolated, and the local people do not identify with Aberdaron (the nearest larger village) in the same way that Cwm people identify with Penmachno.[1] This was confirmed by our findings concerning membership of voluntary organizations and by the people chosen to organize a local carnival or fête. People's choices in this respect recognized no natural barrier between Penmachno and Cwm, and while people from both settlements selected people from the village other than their own, the informal leadership was in fact concentrated in Cwm. In our wish to look at differences between the two settlements in terms of the density of second homes we may well have set up an artificial barrier between them because, despite the considerably higher density of ownership in Cwm, most people we talked to did not differentiate between the two.

At the other end of the scale some villages in North Wales with a fairly low density of second homes, such as Llansannan, still exhibit a wide variety of voluntary associations and organizations and a fairly high degree of membership drawn from the village itself and the surrounding area. The level of hostility towards second homes and their owners as measured in Chapter 7 was higher in Llansannan than in Rhiw, Penmachno and Cwm. An interesting point in this respect concerns the recent proposal by a Cheshire property company to develop a site of just over six acres near the centre of the village for the construction of thirty-four houses. Outline planning permission was refused by the former Denbighshire County Council in February 1974 on the grounds that the development would be alien to the character and social structure of the village, that the relatively high rate of completion would be in direct contrast to normal gradual evolution, and that there was no demand for such speculative building. The company's appeal against this decision was heard in the village community centre in late 1975 and was attended by thirty or so local residents. The company's claim that only people wishing to contribute something to the village and to be absorbed into the community would buy the houses, and that their intention was to stagger the construction of the houses over a number of years according to demand, was countered by the clerk to the community council who argued that a large influx of non-Welsh-speaking incomers would alter the Welsh character and the balance of the village. It seems that the proposal, which will increase the housing stock of the village itself by some 28% is still in the balance. Formal opposition to a more easily indentifiable development will be easier to generate than opposition to the more piecemeal encroachment of second-home ownership, but this example does show an awareness on the part of local people of the Welsh character of the area, and a concern that it should resist the immigration of people with a different linguistic and cultural background.

It is likely then that hypothesis two will hold for areas of low and very high density in that where the traditional lifestyle still manifests itself people will react with hostility towards what they regard as an encroachment on it and a potential threat to it. But there will be a level of second-home ownership in the presence of which in the final analysis local services will be forced to close, while those organizations and institutions which are manifestations of the traditional way of life will, in the face of declining membership, likely follow suit. Within this range, however, the position is more problematic. As far as the present study is concerned Croesor and Penmachno exhibit medium density second-home ownership, although this density is somewhat greater in the former, which is spatially a smaller settlement. Both villages have experienced quarry closures in past years, although these were completed somewhat earlier in Croesor and the presence of English incomers has been a feature of the Croesor area for longer. The prevailing pattern of attitudes is more hostile in Croesor towards second homes and their owners than in Penmachno and although this difference as measured by the semantic differential is not significant statistically it may be that because of their historical experience, because of their history of nationalism or because of the size of the village, the people of Croesor are in fact more hostile to the phenomenon of second-home development.

Certainly the concerns for the language and for the Welshness of the village were present fifteen years ago. An interesting work by Philip O'Connor published in 1962 contains the passage:

> Emrys Williams, farmer, with a voice in which nostalgia for times past sounded like cellos said 'It's not as it used to be up here now' . . . I said: 'It's changed a lot?' . . . 'Quite a lot'. The village, said Mr. Williams 'gets smaller and smaller'. It would become a holiday place – 'and the community will be finished by then, and it's the same everywhere I'm afraid. There was quote a good community here . . . There's nearly none at all now. And we're very disturbed about that. We feel strongly . . . I'd like the Welsh language to stay, if it can. And if more English people

are coming here, well then there's no hope of the Welsh language, it will die out, yes. And then there won't be any mention of the poor old Welsh – the language will die out . . . You lose quite a lot when you lose the language you know.'[2]

Of the Welsh leaving and the English coming another resident opines:

'It's really our own fault that they are leaving. As Welsh people we're not trying to anything about it. We're just moving into the council houses and the English people are moving into the cottages and into the farmsteads . . . the young men have to drift away and find other work, and the families naturally drift away with them.'[3]

An important consideration presents itself here. The effects of second-home ownership on a receiving area will depend to a great extent on the actual prevailing structure of the community concerned, both in terms of an existing level of second-home ownership and in terms of the ability of the area to maintain a level of services and of institutional and voluntary organization which is sufficient to 'keep people in'. This will to some extent depend on its size. Clearly the greater number and variety of organizations and associations to be found in Llansannan and Penmachno compared with Rhiw and Croesor is due not only to the relatively smaller proportion of the population that is second-home owners or permanent English residents but also to the larger absolute size of their populations. The Caernarfonshire report on second homes delineates two types of area in the county which it regards as most at risk from the incursions of second homes. These are:[4]

(1) Major settlements and large villages: in popular tourist areas where there is a local housing demand.
(2) Small villages and hamlets: in popular tourist areas or attractive in themselves but where local housing demand is small.

It is felt that in the former the demand for second homes can be high and that large numbers of conversions to second homes would erode community life and reduce the resident population. Such a situation could jeopardise essential services, especially in winter, not only to the settlement itself but also to the wider area it serves. Growth in the number of second homes in the second type of area is argued to present the greatest problems. Once a significant proportion of the housing stock becomes second homes the sense of community begins to disappear and services and shops are reduced and eventually close. Llansannan would be more akin to settlements in the former category while Rhiw and Croesor would be in the latter. It was noted in Chapter 6 that the most frequently voiced objection to second homes in Croesor was that they make it difficult for local people to get houses. A number of examples of the difficulties encountered by local people in this respect were recounted during our field work, in sharp contrast to the views of some respondents in Rhiw who felt that there was no local demand for houses at all. Such examples in Croesor, whether or not the recounting of the same story by a number of people and whether or not the result of the policy of the local landowner, will be more easily identified in such smaller areas and will lead to a certain amount of suspicion and hostility.

In this way, then, factors peculiar to a particular area may well have an important influence on the views of local people towards second-home ownership, factors which, despite other similarities, may not be repeated in other areas, and they may serve to concentrate attention on particular effects of social change in particular areas. It was noted in Chapter 4 that the geographical separation of second-home properties from those still occupied by all-year-round residents has not occurred in the villages that form the basis of this study to the extent that it has done between properties occupied by incomers and native residents in some of the commuter villages in South East England. This is an important consideration in the light of the opposition to the proposed development in Llansannan. Where such geographical separation does occur it is possible that the findings of Pahl in terms of the growing awareness on the part of local people of national class divisions will be repeated because of the easier identification involved and the characteristics that would be attributed to the 'people of the new houses', be they second-home owners or all-year-round residents. Where such estates were second-home estates they would not necessarily be monuments to economic decline, for purpose-built developments would not require an original out-movement of population to vacate second homes. This leads on to the second main concern of this chapter – an attempt to outline some avenues for further research to follow.

The researcher who is concerned with gaining some comparative under-standing of the types and degree of community involvement on the parts of local and non-local people can choose between:

(1) The traditional community study approach which seeks to achieve a comprehensive account of all the major institutions, activities and relations within a single locality.

(2) The singling out for investigation of an institution which is regarded as particularly important for the understanding of community and the change it has undergone.

It has been widely recognized that the chapel in terms of formal religious organization and its associated activities once served as a community centre in that it provided a spiritual focus of integrating values as well as a centre of social activities within a locality. Attachment to a religious congregation was closely associated with community and family identity and in North Wales religious organizations continued until recently to virtually monopolize organized social life. Identification of the characteristics of the religiously active and non-active, and their conceptions of and orientations towards the locality, can therefore be expected to add to our understanding of the community in North Wales, its adaptation in the face of, and its resilience to, change. However, the findings of the present study, in common with those of a number of others in rural Wales, suggest that as far as the participation of non-local people is concerned community involvement, if it does indeed exist, is unlikely to be manifested in the religious domain, except perhaps in terms of the benefit of the church and the detriment of the chapel. This is primarily a result of the barrier of the Welsh language in Welsh-speaking areas which will deter even the most religiously committed monoglot English speaker. Whether English people do not attend because services are held in Welsh or whether they are held in Welsh because English people do not attend is indeed problematic, but we were told that English people in Llansannan had failed in their attempt to get services held in English in one of the chapels.

Consequently, although an examination of the religious domain will provide an account of the social context of religious activity and the place of religion within the contemporary institutional framework of the locality, as well as indicating the adaptation and resistance to change that is present, it will not add greatly to our understanding of relations between incomers, especially second-homers, and local people.

The sociology of community has provided us with a number of paired concepts for classifying orientations to the community, and these include, for example, 'local/cosmopolitan', 'established/outsider', and 'traditional/non-traditional'. If we accept that the phenomenon of second-home development in rural Wales is a manifestation of social change, and that attitudes and responses towards this phenomenon are attitudes and responses to social change and towards the social change that this phenomenon causes, then the paired concepts suggest that we look at the context of second-home development in rural Wales as two-fold, involving the 'Locality' and the 'Nation'. We can hypothesize that a relationship exists between conceptions of and attitudes towards locality and attitudes towards second homes as social change. For this it will be necessary to incorporate the structural elements in the locality situation which will affect attitudes and orientations towards the locality. Pahl, and Bell and Newby, have argued that the view of 'the village in the mind' held by newcomers differs from the village as it actually is and from the village as perceived by local people. Thus we can hypothesize that the structural position of local people and that of non-locals will differ to the extent of generating different concepts of locality which will lead to differing attitudes to social change and to second-home development.

Apart from differences in the structural positions of incomers and established there will also be differences in the existing structures of various second-home owner localities. For example, the institutional background to social life in Llansannan is quite different from that in Rhiw, and this will provide another variable upon which attitudes to social change may depend. There will, then, apart from differences between people according to their structural positions within a particular locality, be differences according to structural differences occurring between villages, which may be influenced to a greater or lesser degree by the extent and density of second-home ownership in the locality.

There will be a separate set of influences associated with the possession or non-possession of characteristics which we can call 'a nationalistic Welsh character'. These will cut across the local/non-local divide so that the attitudes of a person characteristically 'locally oriented' to the locality may in fact be more importantly the product of the set of characteristics that we have called 'a nationalistic Welsh character', a crude index for which may be called 'attitudes towards and conceptions of anglicisation'. This in turn enables us to hypothesize that conceptions of and attitudes towards anglicisation will comprise an important part of attitudes towards social change and towards its manifestation in terms of second-home ownership. This two-level relationship will form the basis for an analysis of differences in the attitudes of local and non-local people, and between those of people living in different areas towards social change as it is manifested by second homes.

If responses to second-home ownership are essentially responses towards social change, the evaluation of change will vary according to the position the individual takes up in relation to the 'traditional Welsh way of life'. Isabel Emmett, in her Study of a North Wales Village, says that:

> 'In Llan, Buchedd A and Buchedd B are not separate. At a superficial glance the division appears to be there' . . . but . . . 'Unlike Jenkins' Buchedd A people, most of them value Wales more than they value worldly achievement; they would rather see their sons shovelling manure or working in the factory than see them go to London . . . for these and for others who could send their children "farther on" the community wins. The fact that intelligent, well-informed people have stayed in the community in the past means that the community is worth staying in now.' [5]

The 'almost Buchedd A' people in Llan see their fellows 'not in the main as an opposing group but as individuals . . . The frequent presence of English visitors . . . makes Llan people very aware of their Welshness. In the presence of the enemy, Welshness is the primary value; deacon and drunkard are friends, old schisms become unimportant.'[6] This transformation, if indeed transformation there has been, may be seen as impinging upon the localism/nationalism divide and may help our understanding of differences in attitudes and responses to second-home development. Emmett in fact argues that 'the English take the place of the upper, upper-middle or ruling class, and nationalism is the dress in which class antagonisms are expressed',[7] and this may influence the development of the awareness of national class divisions as a consequence of the presence of the incomers.

The importance of the localism/nationalism divide **is** that if we are concerned with change and attitudes towards it, attitudes towards change are bound to constrain and in the longer period influence the social and economic effects of change. In this respect the nationalist/non-nationalist and local/non-local divide is an important starting point. It is a means of access to the important implications of second-home development in relation to both the social and the economic aspects of planning and development. The effects **of** second-home development on the receiving area depend to a great extent on the actual prevailing structure of the community concerned, such that there exists a need to look at the community closely in the first place, for the effects in one area will differ from those in another. One way in which the roots of this difference can be approached is in terms of the local/non-local and nationalist/non-nationalist framework.

An important concern of further research into the effects of second-home ownership on the receiving community would be to understand the attitudes and orientations of those who are spatially linked, which could be approached in terms of socio-metric or network analysis (in terms say of friendship or contact, or self-help and co-operation) and a recognized attitude scaling procedure (if this were needed). In this way the structural elements of the locality situation could be made more explicit and in this respect the investigation of a particularly salient institution in terms of membership or congregation would make the conceptualization process easier. If the phenomenon of second-home ownership in Welsh rural areas is considered to be a topic worthy of study then it must be regarded as a manifestation of, and approached in terms of, social change. It is clearly difficult to isolate second-home ownership as a variable because of the other agents of social change which will be operating, but if we accept the view that, rather than being the cause or the symptom, second-home ownership is more an added complication of social and economic decline, then it will be an agent of social change.

In any event it is hoped that the present study, limited though its scope has been, will help to stimulate further study, if only through its mistakes.

REFERENCES

(1) See LLOYD, M. G. and THOMASON, G. F. (1963), *Welsh Society in Transition*, The Council of Social Service for Wales and Monmouthshire, for a discussion of the clearer divisions between the village community and the surrounding agricultural community in areas which border on the sea (p. 9).

(2) O'CONNOR, P. (1962), *Living in Croesor*, Hutchinson, London. p. 84.

(3) IBID, p. 85.

(4) PYNE, C. B. (1972), op. cit., pp. 53–58.

(5) EMMETT, I. (1964), op. cit., p. 12.

(6) IBID, p. 13.

(7) IBID, p. 23.

APPENDIX

THE SEMANTIC DIFFERENTIAL

The semantic differential is a technique for the refined measurement of semantic connotations. Its purpose is to evaluate the meaning of given terms to individuals or groups of individuals. The test provides a standardizing assessment of meaning, allowing comparisons of the meaning of concepts to be made between given individuals and groups. It evolved from a theory of meaning put forward by Osgood, Suci and Tannenbaum (1957)[1] who stated that the meanings which individuals have for the same sign vary to the extent that their behaviour towards that sign has varied, because the meaning of the sign is totally dependent on the nature of behaviour occurring when that sign is being established. They argue that, given the essential 'sameness' of human organisms and the stability of physical laws, the most primary perceptual signs should be quite constant across individuals, while, given the stability of learning experience within a particular culture, the meaning of most common verbal signs will be highly similar. Conversely the meanings of many signs will reflect the idiosyncracies of individual experience.

Osgood, Suci and Tannenbaum give three prerequisites for the implementation of the semantic differential test:

(1) A carefully devised sample of alternative verbal responses which can be standardized across subjects.

(2) These alternatives are to be elicited not emitted so that encoding fluency is eliminated as a variable.

(3) These alternatives are to be representative of the way in which meanings vary.

To increase the sensitivity of the semantic differential a scale is inserted between each pair of bi-polar adjectives so that respondents can indicate the intensity and direction of each judgement they make of a concept. A considerable body of literature exists concerning the semantic differential technique and when responses to concepts using the test have been repeatedly factor-analysed three predominant factors have been extracted. These are:

    i. The evaluative factor.

    ii. The activity factor.

    iii. The potency factor.

It is generally accepted that the major property of attitudes is that they are predispositions to act in an evaluative manner because they are learned and implicit. They are potentially bi-polar in that they are favourable or unfavourable, and they may show behavioural tendencies of approach or avoidance. Attitudes can therefore be seen as a part of the internal mediation activity that operates between stimulus and response. Repeated factor analyses of semantic differential tests have shown the evaluative factor to be dominant, and it is becoming widely used as an economical instrument of attitude measurement. It is often necessary, however, to use scales other than the evaluative in order to obscure the purpose of measurement as far as the respondent is concerned and to provide further information as to the meaning of the concept as a whole.

In the present study the semantic differential test was compiled using eleven seven-point scales, chosen from lists presented by Osgood *et al.*, which represented all three factors, the evaluative, activity and potency dimensions of meaning. The following seven adjectival pairs were selected as having high evaluative loadings:

FRIENDLY ....UNFRIENDLY
SUCCESSFUL ...........................UNSUCCESSFUL
GOOD ....BAD
IMPORTANT ....UNIMPORTANT
CO-OPERATIVE..........................UNCO-OPERATIVE
NECESSARY ....UNNECESSARY
RICH ....POOR

Three pairs were selected with high activity loadings:

ACTIVE................................PASSIVE
GROWING ....DIMINISHING
NEW ....OLD

And one pair with a high potency loading was chosen:

STRONG ....WEAK

The following nine concepts were selected to be judged by respondents on these scales:

SECOND HOMES
SECOND-HOME OWNERS
ENGLISHNESS
TOURISM
PUBLIC HOUSE
WELSHNESS
THE WELSH LANGUAGE
LOCAL PEOPLE
CHAPEL

Respondents were asked to mark the point representing their judgement of the relationship of the concept and the adjectival pair on the seven-point bi-polar scale.

A number of important points need to be made concerning the suitability of the semantic differential test for the present study of second homes.

(1) Some scales, particularly those with high evaluative loadings, can assume different meanings in the context of different concepts, and research has shown that some concepts have two or three evaluative factors which reflect different shades of evaluative meaning. This possibility of more than one evaluative factor is accepted in the present study, but the test was not scored with scale weightings because we were primarily engaged in a simple exercise to identify the attitudes of those affected by second-home development rather than to define some of the more abstruse shades of meaning of some of the concepts involved. Even so, possible discrepancy between evaluative factors must be acknowledged.

(2) Validity does not have the same significance for attitude tests as for other tests. Attitudes are usually readily accessible and face validity is often taken as satisfactory. Even where this is not the case the fact that there is no necessary relationship between attitudes and overt behaviour and the fact that attitudes can change relatively quickly pose problems for the establishment of reliability and validity. However, satisfactorily high test-retest coefficients have been reported by Osgood *et al.* Reliability is especially evident with the evaluative factor which essentially measures like and dislike and which forms the larger focus of the present study. Further, high correlations which have been obtained between the semantic differential and other attitude scales are accepted as being indicative of validity.

(3) The semantic differential test itself does not consider the attitude situation and it has little bearing on everyday life. Nevertheless it is possible for a person to have an attitude towards an object irrespective of his or her situation in relation to the object.

(4) The scaling of the semantic differential technique assumes integer scores at equal intervals. The important considerations are direction and intensity, the first qualitative, the second quantitative. Some research has indicated that polarity scores should not be directly related to or equated with intensity, and it has been argued that intensity should be measured independently. Recognizing this

limitation, in the present study the polarization of responses is used to signify both intensity and direction.

In view of the generally satisfactory background of the semantic differential as a measure of attitudes and the care taken to ensure that the test was maximally valid for all respondents, it is reasonable to feel confident in the results emanating from the test.